Life, Lines And Rhymes
(mostly by Mark Fishman)

*Lines and Lyrics through the years..... and where to find
them under their very loose themed affiliations.*

Intro To The Poetic Motherlode

People

(In Three Chapters - Work, Problems And Problems With Technology).

People And Work

People And Problems

Lost Love

(And Lost Lust)

Age And Passing

Intro To The Poetic Motherlode

This is what people are saying about a 'Life, Lines And Rhymes'......

"I loved the quotes - it's amazing what he's done with copy and paste"
An imaginary friend.

"If you enjoy books with page numbers then this is one for you"
A friend of my imaginary friend who lives next door.

"A great dose of morbid introspection topped off with lashings of unhealthy cynicism - if you love poetry..... steer clear"
Someone my imaginary friend knows (who's imaginary).

"I couldn't wait .....to get to the end!- thank God it had one"
My science fiction other self - also imaginary.

Instructions for use:

1. Open book
2. Choose poem
3. Read to yourself or aloud
4. Stop half way
5. Yawn

6. Close book
7. Make note to do something else next time
8. Pick up again, once you've forgotten the note.

Welcome to this poetic emporium …..

Where you'll find poems….
- That are a couple of verses too long
- Or just go on and on and on
- Would better suit being in a song
- Sound mixed up and wrong
- Aren't clear where the writer is coming from
- Some are about love and the human condition
- Some are about Kings, Queens and politicians
- Some are about events and history
- Some are about conspiracies and mysteries
- Or popular stars and their showbiz empresarios
- In the most fantastic and fictional scenarios
- Some are about religion and one's about football
- Some just don't make any sense at all
- Some are ok, rhyme and jog along
- And some just aren't worth the paper or drive they're written on.

These are the things I should have said but I couldn't
These are the things I could have said but I didn't
They will always exist outside of me
They will always exist in spite of me
They are chronicles, tales and reflections in time

They are naked moments and they are mine.

<u>Reader warning</u>
It's not an area I excel in
So apologies in advance for any bad grammar and
spelling.

Parents may find some material unsuitable for children...well anyone really. Contains one or more of the following: (S) swearing/expletives, (P) references to politicians, (HR) half rhymes and (HFSS) high fat /
sugar content confectionery references.

Let the journey begin….

"Let me take you down because I'm going to…."
John Lennon 1967.

People

(In Three Chapters - Work, Problems And Problems With Technology).

People And Work

(1) A Tube Of Smarties - an Oldfield/Fishman collab - 1981 (page 14)

I go to work in a tube of smarties
Candy coated arty fartiec
Cardboard smiles and pinstripe suits
And girls that look like opal fruits
They spend their days displayed in trays
With their caramel habits and milky ways
Their only thought and only treat
Is to have a big house on Quality Street.

My hard-boiled boss in the office at night
Chained to the desk and his Turkish delight
His wife number crunching with pencil and pad
Finding a hole in the mint they once had
He's secretly spying the dolly mixtures
Looking to fill up some empty fixtures
Some bounty hunters some married twice
Some of them searching for paradise.

I come home after eight
Why am I always late?
Too many drinks after work
With people that think I'm a jerk
Each one with a pocket full of poses
Breathing through their toffee noses.

I go to work in a tube of smarties
I meet them again at office parties
Liquorice lipstick on milk chocolate faces

Acid drop comments in all the right places
Taking sweeteners and sipping slush
Always looking for the next sugar rush
Stuck in the jam, drowned in the crush
Treacle people just like us.

(2) Taking Stock (Loose Change) -1985 (page 15)

He took stock of the matter
He knew he had lost interest
His marriage was in tatters
He had nothing left to invest.

On no account could he leave her
What would they say at the bank?
But he couldn't bear to see her
So he stayed out late and drank.

His late night speculations
Often led to a rented flat
Where he forgot his station
In a joint venture on the mat.

She the other party
Mortgaged off her love
She lured him with Bacardi
And black patent leather gloves.

This was a foreign exchange
But with some tender feelings
This she found most strange
A first in her trade dealings.

He wanted more than a share

He bid for a take over
He thought about her everywhere
Loving and loathing her.

But how do you break the bonds
Of the family trust?
The wife and kids get conned
For unrequited lust.

Then there was the big bang
Truth in a bear market
The ruin of their finance plan
Love? - they'd have to park it.

His wife received the lot
Plus tax on capital gains
If the penny ever drops
He'll know he was to blame.

He pays a monthly allowance
Which she spends on Chardonnay
She drinks and then she counts
The loose change left to save.

(3) Bread Winners - 1989 (page 16)

Give us this day our daily bread
Let's collectively hail the breadwinners
Aspiring to be part of the upper crust
They've tired of chip butties and TV dinners
They're going to learn to use their loaves
They won't do anything for anyone
Unless they're getting some dough
You won't catch them loafing around

They are their mother's pride
You won't find them on the bread line
Or on the dole
They might have a bun in the oven
But they're always on a roll
Or rising ahead
The greatest thing since sliced bread.

(4) Great - 2018 (page 17)

He was great
Or so he thought
She was greater
And more greatly sought
Both in great jobs
From great places.
He was from the great beyond
And she the great divide
They went to great lengths
To tell great big lies
They both had great appetites
And had the greatest fun
Going great guns
To buy a great home
With a great big loan
And have great kids
Surrounded by a great wall
And all creatures great and small
They'd both fought in the great war
Outside in the great outdoors
They'd both enjoyed a great depression
Which had left a great impression
They had a great time
And great hobbies

They had great minds
In great bodies
It was no great shakes
They had great poise and charm
Until someone got in the way
Then they'd do them great harm
But even they couldn't avoid
Great disappointment and loss
When at a great cost
They couldn't get a spot
On the Great British Bake off.

He felt lucky to have a great wife
With great pay and great perks
Wearing great clothes
To great concerts and great shows
They had a great future
Together or apart
And if suddenly it came to an end
In trouble and strife
Well they'd have had a great life.

To be honest I found them both a little bit grating.

(5) Running A Business - 2018 (page 18)

Running a business just got easier
Be your own boss
Set your own cost
Cover your own loss
It couldn't be easier.

Leading a team just got simpler
Do your own training

Decide who you're blaming
Conduct your own public shaming
It couldn't be simpler.

Driving sales just got dreamier
Build your own IT
Keep your own inventory
Decide your own redundancies
It couldn't be dreamier.

Communication just got steamier
Create your own straplines
Draw your own red lines
Write your own headlines
It couldn't be steamier.

Taking responsibility just got lovelier
Appearing first in class
Taking everyone to task
Covering your own arse
It couldn't be lovelier.

Happy staff just got happier
Who love being on their knees
Taking their pay freeze
And are so eager to please
They couldn't be happier.

(6) Left Behind - 2020 (page 19)

You've been left ...behind
Behind those with sport utility vehicles and driver controls
Who take summer holidays three times a year to the posh
part of the Costa Del Sol

Who are annually world cruising and live in a rustic semi detached
Plus have a 2nd home in the country, fashionably distressed
and thatched
They have blinkered myopic middle English views
So much uninformed rhetoric from their mouths spews
They are interfering, self opinionated extroverts
Who think life is just like a John Lewis Christmas advert
And they are always keen to boast and mention
Their final salary non contributory pension
They have handmade craft stands in village halls
They exude a progressive liberalism that they won't pay for
but no else one can afford.

You're out of step with them, no longer in line
You used to be right at the front
Now you're left ...behind.

You've been left.... behind
While your colleagues issue a stream of oleaginous
sycophantic corporate posts
Always playing the fawning online community hosts
So subtle, but Machiavellian in nature
Raising their profile and building their stature
Gaining by the dozen extracurricular sinecures
They've got jazz hands and elaborate overtures
They support any initiative or volunteering opportunity
They're the golden girls and boys of the happy clappy committee.

Your fault, you never heeded the warning signs
You used to be right at the front
Now you're left ...behind.

You've been left.... behind

It went still all of a sudden and there was nowhere to run to and nothing
was running
Those in good shape kept plodding along and those who weren't kept
struggling
Closing time, last orders, then happy hour had come and gone
We'd been much too drunk for much too long
We were breaking up, we were on mute, losing connection
Washed away in one global tsunami of mass introspection
Sitting ducks, sitting at home, sitting it out all alone
Waiting to be brought back into the fold, like spies waiting to come in
from the cold.

You've always known how to get there- but not this time
You used to be right at the front
Now you're left ...behind.

You've been left...behind
While the rest of the world had gone online
Your post tray and landline
Got progressively less used over time
You got fewer documents to physically sign
You'd planned to live your life to the full not as one
Now Gen X, Y and Z have more disposable income
No one treating you seriously
As you wear repeatedly
Your shades of mediocrity
You couldn't keep pace with the technological advancements
and fads
And society's heavy reliance on mobile phones and Ipads
None of which you've ever used or had
You're now paying the penalty
For having never understood a desktop PC
What did it mean to stream?

And why no buttons, and what's a touch screen?
And why was no one using a map
And what the hell was sat nav?
Everything seems to require the skills you now so clearly lack
Apart from when vinyl made a comeback.

You came from a world where the pencil and pen were king
A world built on paper with light horizontal lines
Nobody today values these things
Sometimes the world can just be so unkind
You used to be right at the front
Now you're left ...behind.

(7) Make Or Break - 2020 (page 22)

Breaking up, breaking falls
Making money, making love
Breaking bread, breaking records
Making babies, making up
Breaking thunder, breaking bones
Making time, making amends
Breaking clouds, breaking homes
Making wine and making friends.

Breaking windows, breaking doors
Making waves, making cakes
Breaking silence, breaking sores
Making out, making mistakes
Breaking fingers, breaking toes
Making plans, making a face
Break a leg and break your nose
Making peace, making a case.

It doesn't matter how much you break

Everyone is on the make.

Breaking vows, breaking laws
Making noise, making calls
Breaking friendships, breaking jaws
Making good, making rules
Breaking out, breaking in
Making meals, making bread
Breaking down, breaking wind
Making out then making beds.

Making an effort, making the day
Breaking glasses, breaking sweat
Making certain, making way
Breaking open another bottle of Claret
Making demands, making me think
Breaking news, breaking joints
Making a pass, making a drink
Breaking bad's breaking points.

Sometimes you break down and just despair
And wonder what they're making over there.

Making wills, making sense
Breaking fast, breaking tears
Making signs, making comments
Breaking habits, breaking clear
Making peace, making war
Breaking things, breaking deals
Making safe, making sure
Breaking backs and braking wheels.

It doesn't matter how much you break

Everyone is on the make.

It's not a deal breaker
Because sooner or later
We're all going to meet our maker
And if you can break on through
It just might be the making of you

OMG....I need to make a break for it

(8) Champions Of Skullduggery - 2021 (page 24)

We can do it cheaply
And very discreetly
We guarantee delivery
Of increased productivity
And reduced inefficiency
It's exactly
What you need
But they'll be
Unavoidably
Just a few casualties
To pay for this opportunity
To drive greater customer advocacy
Via headcount flexibility
And yes some redundancies
But we'll help you act responsibility
To protect trading continuity
Whilst retaining wallet loyalty
Removing your dependency
On a commercial liability
That's employee inability
To deliver things successfully
Both physically and mentally

Failing regrettably
To step up effectively
To the goals created centrally
Which are now completed technically
Removing all complexity
By automating directly
And integrating seamlessly
With digital capabilities.

Market forces unavoidably
Have increased the probability
Of reduced profitability
So you have to act speedily
And sadly make redundancies
Which we will handle sensitively
Addressing most professionally
And almost always honestly
With a degree of ambiguity
And maybe an apology
But we won't overplay the pleasantries
This was going to happen eventually
We'll make our case convincingly
It'll hold its own statistically
They can't challenge our credibility
As we always know best generally
We have innate infallibility
And core business case supremacy
We're the captains of our industry
The champions of skullduggery.

(9) WTF?-2022 (page 25)

You know you've got the upper hand
Since you put a nail in our foot of pride

Don't blame the hand of fate
You're the one with something to hide
You tell us again and again how much you care
But it's just one more stylish outfit from your wardrobe of platitudes
To hide your self righteous behaviour
To mask those cynical attitudes
You're not listening, we think you must be deaf
WTF?

Same old thing in brand new drag
Comes sweeping in bold and vain
As ugly as a political millionaire
Opening a bottle of their own celebratory champagne
One more excruciating team day
One more vision and strategy
This is a crime by any other name
Like robbery, assault and battery
How many more times can you say the same thing over and over
It's shameful, it's repetitive, it's indecent overexposure
How can something so shallow be so overdressed ?
WTF?

Another magnificent overspend
On consultants, slides and soundbites
To convert the new disciples
And find the new proselytes
Who will repeat the newly paid for mantras
Like "We shall overcome"
You don't give a damn for what went before
It's this way to Jerusalem
And yet underneath this flannel, the spin and the gift wrap
We swear as we get closer it smells like the same old pile of crap
When did you start pointing right and no longer to the left?

WTF?

We wouldn't really mind so much
If we'd seen some positive change
And things were moving forward
Not heading backwards again
Your message is so over spun and over engineered
We think you might protest too much - is it out of fear?
Our general lack of feedback is not a sign we feel inspired
We're strategically on our knees, worn out,trashed and tired
We think you're mad or having a laugh
To keep tiptoeing up your critical path
So much time and energy and for so little just reward
There must be a law against this
We just don't know what it's called
Is it trickery, or hyperbole, or perhaps it's really theft
WTF?

.... and after the business has taken what it can take
You'll get a brown envelope or a golden handshake
A reward for your incompetence and to save some face
As someone equally not qualified is ready to take your place
With a new plan to burn the remaining cash that's left
WTF?

At the Board meeting...

What's the plan, Stan?
Where's the agenda, Brenda?
When's the spin, Tim?
Have we got a scheme, Jean?
Show me the strategy, Natalie
What's the cost, Ross?

Does it wash its face, Grace?
Is there a return, Vern?

(10) The Elephant In The Room - 2022 (page 28)

Another day in the office
Harassed and stressed
Impossible deadlines to meet
But I was doing my best
Then an urgent message from upstairs
Stop what you're doing and grab a chair
I put down the pastry that I'd just bought
And ran up to the next floor for a trading talk
I joined the discussion on making advances
In these challenging economic circumstances
With an IPad resting on my lap
I heard how we'd win our customers back
Move from bust, to bold, then boom
But then suddenly I saw the elephant in the room.

It was grey and scary
And looking right at me
I felt my mounting anxiety
I put my hand up instantly
To flag this issue immediately
My boss didn't like ever being interrupted
Or having his meeting inelegantly disrupted
I described in detail this big grey problem
It wasn't one you came across very often
My colleagues listened attentively
They were supportive and acted sensitively
But the truth and unwelcome reality
They really all questioned my sanity

Not believing what I thought was easy to perceive
They all hoped soon I'd exit and leave
Not one of them was over the moon
Hearing about the elephant in the room.

I said "..we couldn't just let it roam free
It was a big issue as far as I could see
Someone has to decide what to do
This elephant wasn't just big, it was huge
We need to cage it up and take it to a zoo
Or else it will trample over me and you
Or send it back to where it came from
But in this meeting it certainly doesn't belong"
I couldn't understand how my colleagues ignored
A problem so big it might not get through the door
But unfortunately it was invisible to them
And my bosses, acquaintances and friends
Why couldn't they see what was in front of their eyes
So after the meeting and the end of day goodbyes
I decided I'd take care that late afternoon
Of the elephant in the room.

I invited it to tea with the family
They were surprised at its size and immensity
Fortunately the elephant for them was visible
And they could see it was making me miserable
It dominated everything we did
It wasn't something you could keep well hid
It was there with us while we ate out supper
It would never let us rest or from this strange day recover
It was part of every conversation we had
By the end of the day it was driving us mad
The kids told me this elephant had got to go

It was filling our family with too much woe
And I should take it back to work the next day
It was a big fat problem and it needed to go away
The only way to remove my worrying gloom
Was for everyone to acknowledge the elephant in the room.

My wife said "......if we painted it a different colour
It will still look like an elephant but perhaps unlike any other
Then friends from work might finally see
What's so obvious to you and me"
So I painted it yellow, red and blue
Painted it every conceivable colour and hue
When it was done I couldn't wait to tell her
As it was a much brighter looking fella
So bright it just might overwhelm her
I'm now thinking of calling it Elma
It looked like a technicolour dream
Unlike any other elephant that had ever been seen
No one at work could fail to view
What was no longer grey, opaque or see through
It was a great big multi shaded mammal
No longer obscured by waffle or flannel
We could now all work together and very soon
Sort the elephant in the room.

I took the elephant through the office doors
Could it be seen? I still wasn't sure
I got it to the fourth but it weighed a ton
Another trading meeting had just begun
I opened the door with hesitation
Not sure if my colleagues would show any appreciation
For their meeting being interrupted once again
And reintroduced to my great troublesome pain

But to my great delight it was evident
They all could now see the elephant!
No longer was it just my problem to resolve
Now everyone could get involved
I was so pleased it wasn't just me
Taking this problem seriously.

I've learnt when I see an elephant next time
And people think I'm out of my mind
It doesn't mean I'm quite insane
It just means we don't see things the same
Then I'll make sure I spend time supporting the team
By painting the elephant red, blue, yellow and green
So for everyone it's accepted and seen
I'll no longer take for granted and assume
Everyone can see the elephant in the room.

People And Problems

(11) Stepping Out - 1984 (page 31)

She takes a deep breath before ascending the scales
Removes all her clothing and then she exhales
Her disappointments are ever so real
Wonders why her body never gets a fair deal.

It's Saturday night and she's going out
To a place where you're expected to pose and pout
She's feeling apprehensive and she's feeling afraid
She regrets all the good looking friends that she's made.

She thinks her legs are too short and her thighs are too big
It's been that way since she was a kid

She watches her diet but that makes it worse
And good looking girls she'll silently curse.

She'll paint on the charm and hope it will cure
All the apprehension she has to endure
She's tried all the fads and none of them work
She exercises like a physical jerk
All in the hope her body will be blessed
And she'll feel ready to dress and impress.

....but it never happens it's always the same
On the edge of her bed looking for someone to blame
That's when it's bad and she's on the rocks
Staying in and overdosing on Dairy Box.

She wanted to be the one and only
Instead she feels let down and lonely
She's only happy in her dreams
Away from the disappointing, dull and routine
But she knows this is an act of folly
And that's why she feels so melancholy.

But don't we also feel the same?
We're not as confident as we claim
Aren't we also ravaged by self doubt?
Staying in when we should be stepping out.

(12) Where Does This Book End? - 1985 (page 32)

Where does this book end?
Out on loan or on the shelf
Or in the hands of Mr Right
A charming man of good manners and wealth.

Where does this book end?
She can't remember how it started
Now stuck behind a library desk
Abandoned and cold hearted.

Where does this book end?
She's only got to chapter three
Where the willing heroine with the loving heart
Meets her handsome hero, all dapper and smart.

Where does this book end?
Perhaps in a club or singles bar
Or on a holiday for the over forties
Where talk is cheap and the jokes are naughty.

And every night she files away
The yellow pages of a life miscarried
That itemise and diarise
Her fading desire to be loved and married.

Where does this book end?
She wonders when she'll turn a corner
There must be something more to life
Than keeping things in alphabetical order.

Where does this book end?
Perhaps at the back of her Filofax
She can organise till her face is blue
But it's not a guarantee that her dreams will come true.

And every night she files away
The tired yellow pages so plain and dour
That regulate and equalise

The losses and failings of a fading wallflower.

Many years later...

When does this book end?
She told me what her story was about
One of fear, frustration and doubt
When all she'd ever wanted was to be stepping out.

(13) Snowbound 2003 (page 34)

The snow fell ....
..and we could not cope
The lunar landscape
Intrigued us and fatigued us
It broke systems
And bent rules
....and we could not cope
It was safer to stay at work and not leave
With a slice of toast and a warm cup of tea
Fearing our cars may have disappeared
In blankets of ice from front to rear
We called loved ones on mobile phones
Warning them we would not be home
We heard stories of wild daring
Six hour journeys home
With the blizzard tearing
At forms we believed were sure and true
Like motorways and gritting crews
We felt overexposure
As our world froze over
...and we could not cope
Lorries skidding into the cars of our colleagues
Emergency services on the M25 trying to blowtorch the

freeze
We live in an age so unused to disaster
That just a bit of bad news from the weather forecaster
Can break our shell of order like porcelain and plaster
And we watch it play out on an analogue stage
Prompting outpourings of panic and rage.

A girl my age came back in tears
A fight had broken out on the flyover
As a car skidded into another car's rear
This night had loosened the bands of control
As the snow fell and the wind rolled
Cars abandoned on cold hard shoulders
The occupants drifting into the dark ether in fright
What made them take flight?
And leave the sanctuary of the four wheel drive
Disappear into the oblivion of the cold hopeless night
To fumble, to tread, to grope
To find help or a way to cope?

(14) England vs France Euro 2004 (page 35)

I can't believe I'm doing this again
That I'm watching this field of elation and pain
The anticipation at the start
As the ball departs
From the foot of Michael Owen
In the first three minutes there's no way of knowing
Where this game will be going
As Rooney takes a run
At Fabien Barthez's goal
And Beckham passes surely
First to Heskey
Then to Cole

The French seem permanently at our end
It's driving me around the emotional bend
I get despondent and have another beer
Someone needs to kick that ball out of here!!
Then a Beckham free kick which we know the French fear
It turns, it bends, catches Vassell's head..it's just in ..and then the
cheers!!
One up against the best team north of Toulouse
But in the 2nd half don't cruise (remind them Sven).

The French come out fighting
And the tension heightens
Our defenders take a pounding
Their full-backs we start hounding
Then Rooney makes a break
Past one player then another
The French defenders can't cover
The pace he's found
In their penalty box
...and he's brought down.

An expectant cheer in the air
"Penalty" whispered everywhere
And there it is - screams of delight
As Beckham steps up in the stadium spotlight
This his forte, this is where he excels
The nation feels its collective heart swell
If he can dip into the nether reaches of his soul
We do believe he'll get a goal
The world stops for 5 seconds
Barthez dives ....and Barthez saves
Now for the cold water of reality
Beckham has fluffed his penalty.

I can't believe it, it can't be true
Beckham's shot did not get through
Barthez jumped to attention
And luckily for the French in the same direction
As the penalty kick Beckham had just taken.

20 minutes to go
Can England hold on?
The fans chorale in rising song
15 minutes, 10 minutes, 5 minutes to go
A fantastic headline is ready to roll.

But....
Heskey fouls a French player
Giving away a free kick
Outside our goal area
Zinedine Zidane
So good they nearly named him twice
Steps up to take it .. it curves and spins
And then it goes in......:(

Well at least we'll get a point
Until I see
The ball land at the feet of
Thiery Henry
Then David James takes him down
And it's another penalty
But to France
Watch those blue shirts dance
Zidane up again
And boots it into the corner of our net
It's a moment I just want to forget

And finally, game over
Now the truth and the agony
This is another of our footballing tragedies
That's the last England match I'll ever see
..........until the next time.

(15) A New Word 2007 (page 38)

A new word came into my life today
One I had never heard before
It would come to occupy my waking hours
And at night the fabric of my dreams claw
For me, yesterday it did not exist
Not in in my vocabulary or chance remarks
Now I freeze at its mention
A single word can be so hard.

It came uninvited
An unwelcome guest
It was almost a whisper
On a fretful breath
One word, a few syllables
At that point not much else to say
Now a thing of import
And it won't go away.

I struggled with the pronunciation
I couldn't master the inflection
I was nervous about saying it out loud
And fearful of correction
It's possibly of Latin origin
Or maybe closer to home
But now always on my radar
And it won't leave me alone.

A new word came into my life today
And with it new conditions
I hear the word everywhere
I've had to shift and reposition
It's anywhere I search
It's in everything I see
It's always in front of me
With disturbing regularity.

It's turned my world upside down
Changing my everyday perspective and view
I've had to learn to live with it
And all the different things I now must do.

(16) Girl On The Street - 2007 (page 39)

Bone thin complexion behind a powder puff masquerade
A handful of purple pills washed down with warm Lucozade
A baby in one hand, a mobile in the other
She's too old to be this year's model but too young to be a mother.

(17) To Cruise - 2013 (page 39)

To cruise, to glide....or is it really an oxymoron...
...for sharing norovirus with a ship full of morons.

(18) It Was Disney Time Again - 2021 (page 39)

She was no Cinderella
She liked to hang around with dwarves
Keeping her presence low key
Eating poisoned apples
She waited for her Prince to come

But it wasn't like the movie
Instead she met a local boy
A beast and not a beauty
Her white skin and rosy lips
To be honest a little strange
It didn't really matter
It was Disney time again,

The three little pigs
Had made sound investments
They didn't give a Donald Duck
For their friends left in the tenements
They thought they'd acted goofy
For not buying or building a house
They'd come further than their old mates
Pluto and Mickey Mouse
They had a distinguished reputation
They needed to maintain
Always cleaning up the past
It was Disney time again.

Answering difficult questions
On that famous late night show
Lying through his teeth
Just like Pinocchio
Then back at the hotel
With another sleeping beauty
Dressed like a little mermaid
All in the line of duty
Enjoying his Fantasia
And lines of class cocaine
Put it on expenses
It was Disney time again.

There had been a shocking disclosure
The selling of hard candy
Someone on the inside
Had clearly set up Bambi
Was it the Mad Hatter
Or the lady and her tramp
Was it Pocahontas
For Disney trading stamps
Bambi now in Wonderland
Frozen and insane
Shacking up with Alice
It was Disney time again.

He needed peeling off the ceiling
He was off his face and hands
Lost and high forever
That's why they call him Peter Pan
His evenings spent with Wendy
And his search for Captain Hook
Who provided all the medicine
And the pills that he took
The croc was always ticking
Too long in the fast lane
He needed a new place to be sick in
It was Disney time again.

It felt just like a dog's life
For Cruella de Vil
By the age of forty one
Typecast and over the hill
She always played the bad cop
Or the evil queen or witch

She just wanted one occasion
Where she wasn't just a bitch
She'd spoken to her agent
But it was all in vain
So it was back to drowning puppies
It was Disney time again.

Minnie Mouse has it sewn up
With more fan mail than the Pope
Mickey's coming off the bottle
But finding it hard to cope
He rented out protection
From the Three Caleberos
He had more money now
Than the Egyptian pharaohs
His Uncle Walt had left him
The entire theme park chain
But in spite of all his money
It was Disney time again.

(19) I Was Born Angry 2021 (page 42)

I was mad as hell when I came out of the womb
I always start an argument whenever I enter a room
I've got an opinion on everything, whatever the subject
If I don't know what I'm talking about then I'll just fudge it
I always want to be heard, I've got a burning urgency
I was born angry.

I challenge every unfairness in society
Even the ones that never ever impact me
I take a contradictory position, just to cause a row
It doesn't matter what I believe in, I'm always right somehow
I love rising tension and anxiety

I was born angry.

Yes I'm dissatisfied with my position and my place
Why is it always someone else in fortune's warm embrace?
They say the grass isn't always greener on the other side
But it all looks pretty green to me from where I reside
I did mean to hurt you, I'm consumed with jealousy
I was born angry.

I've got anger management issues just like the Incredible
Hulk
When I don't get my own way, I have an incredible sulk
If I'm not arguing then I hang around and skulk
I want it all on my own terms, whatever the result
It's not my fault I'm like this, or my responsibility
I was born angry.

I protest too much to seemingly endless foes
I've become a dab hand at shooting poison arrows
I dance around any subject just like Fred Astaire
Until I've made my point, I just won't leave it there
I go on and on and on and on, for an eternity
I was born angry.

I'm always looking forward to the fall out of a fall out
After which I move on to my next argumentative bout
I love hearing myself and the sound of my own voice
I speak so loudly that I don't have any other choice
I just need to always win, even on a technicality
I was born angry.

(20) Weekend Warrior 2022 (page 43)

She shared a 'self help' book with me

Which she passionately insisted I had to read
She drew my attention to her favourite lines
Which she'd learnt to remember and recite over time
.....″As an old man longs for the light
Or a child reaches for a flower
The worthy must be observant day and night
In their quest to achieve a higher power″
To be honest it all sounded a bit overwrought
But at least she's committed I thought
She loved a bit of speculation
Or some spicy new revelation
She was dead excited when she discovered
Scientology and L. Ron Hubbard
Dan Brown and the Lost series
And environmental conspiracy theories
She was queen of a land called melodrama
Surveying its self indulgent panorama
The crown of martyrdom sits proudly on her head
For saying things that didn't need to be said
It's up to her to challenge our social norms and rules
She's the weekend warrior with a lunch time cause.

She'd underlined another quote in her scholarly tome
Just to further ram her points home
″As the rose reaches for the sun
Or pirates seek out buried treasure
We must continue our search for truth
Against which we must be measured″
She wanted for nothing else
No land or share of corporate wealth
But as Daddy's Trust fund was in good health
She never had to worry about looking after herself
She adopted opinions as though they were children

All in service of the arguments she was building
She loved to be heard quoting
And some cod philosophy promoting
She delighted in gloating and non believers were fools
She's the weekend warrior with a lunch time cause.

Like Cinderella going to the ball
I never felt worthy or able
Could a soul as wretched as me
Sit at her Fair Trade coffee table
Unlike her I can't ignore my failings
Of my features they are my most prevailing
Nothing about her seems suspect
She's multi politically socially correct
No surprise we both concur
I can never be as good as her
She's always there selling pamphlets from community halls
She's the weekend warrior with a lunch time cause.

I met her in a macrobiotic restaurant in Chelsea
We tucked into sushi and a JackFruit burger
I came out feeling a lot more healthy
But to be honest the conversation was murder
She tried to expand my understanding
But I found the whole thing too demanding
I looked interested but I was pretending
And she was awfully condescending
It made me feel as miserable as sin
And she didn't clock I was suffering
No one is going to thank her
For being such a drag anchor
But really she's not much different to me
Another member of the bourgeoisie

Accept she's chained herself to an oil refinery
All she really wants to be
Is an evening news celebrity
Her life to date had been disappointingly cruel
She just wants it to mean something that's all
Not one just spent in and out of college and private school
She's the weekend warrior with a lunch time cause

(21) Events, Events, Events - 2022 (page 46)

Birthdays and workdays
Sundays and Mondays
Bad days and sad days
Good days and mad days
Holidays that follow days
Like springtime bank holidays
Counting the future days
All rushing by in a daze.

Events, events, events - they use up our minutes and hours
Events, events, events - they spring up like weeds and flowers.

Another king's funeral
New Roman numerals
We'll wear something suitable
For someone so notable
The death of a president
Who's passing is heaven sent
For all of the malcontents
Who've lost their innocence.

Events, events, events - they change kingdoms, empires and lands
Events, events, events- they're the cause of rebellious last stands.

Go to the hospital
Needing a physical
As part of a medical
Or just something chemical
Getting the test results
Now needing to consult
This news is such a jolt
An unwelcome lightning bolt.

Events, events, events - some you see coming and some you don't
Events, events, events - some you will want and some you won't.

Events that are planned
Events that aren't planned
Events that are past
Events that don't last.

Starting at nursery
School and university
History and Geography
Probate and property
Drive productivity
As a captain of industry
Then the work anniversary
For being so mercenary
A gold watch then surgery
Death is a certainty.

Events, events, events - they trigger our lows and our highs
Events, events, events - they pinpoint and punctuate lives.

Mornings and afternoons
Weddings and honeymoons

Train station waiting rooms
Trying to log into Zoom
Trips and discoveries
Wouldn't it be lovely
A voyage on the open sea
Record for posterity.

Events, events, events - in photos and pictures and lines
Events, events, events - in verses and lyrics and rhymes.

Midwives and undertakers
Losers and moneymakers
Builders and bakers
Destroyers and creators
Butchers of distinction
Planning our eviction
A threat of extinction
Is not a non fiction.

Events that bring joy
Events that destroy
Events that bring pain
Then happen again.

We tell lies and hypnotise
Then radically terrorise
Expose and commercialise
Package and publicise
What's divine and temporal
We class as ephemeral
Plans and dichotomies
Led by mediocrities.

Events, events, events - we have three score years and ten
Events, events, events - they'll come around again and again.

(22) What's That In The Garden Dad? - 2022 (page 49)

What's that in the garden Dad?
Is it the remains of a pigeon who lost a fight with a cat
Or a poorly struck ball from a threadbare bat
A garden glove on a garden mat
Or something more unpleasant than that.

What's that in the garden Dad?
A barking dog that's being chased by a bear
A drunken nobody's underwear
The Anglican Book of Common Prayer
Or Ginger Rogers and Fred Astaire.

What's that in the garden Dad?
A ticking bomb from World War Two
An abandoned bottle of Irn Bru
An escaped Armadillo from a local zoo
A private detective spying on you.

What's that in the garden Dad?
An empty box of Mcdonald's fries
A half eaten Fray Bentos pie
A plague of annoying noisy flies
Buzzing around a nasty surprise.

What's that in the garden Dad?
A piece of debris from a seven four seven
A broken rung from the ladder to heaven
A pair of old slippers - size eleven
The discarded peel of a half eaten melon.

What's that in the garden Dad?
Is it the four horsemen of the Armageddon?
Yul Bryner and the Magnificent Seven
Paul McCartney or John Lennon
Perhaps it's our cousin called Kevin.

What's that in the garden Dad?
We'll only ask you one more time
We don't mean to be pushy or unkind
But it's next to the shed by the washing line
If you still can't see it, you must be blind.

(23) Get Your Kicks On The A406 - 2022 (page 50)

Well if you ever plan to motor north west
Travel my way, by dual carriageway, it's the best
Get your kicks on the A406.

You can drive from Ealing to Wembley
Via Uxbridge and the Hanger Lane gyratory
Get your kicks on the A406.

Well it goes past IKEA
Neasden is near
Via Brent reservoir
Edgware Road isn't far
It's a northwest adventure
At the Brent Cross shopping centre
Golders Green and Henley's Corner
Get busy I should warn ya
Around Hatch End, Bounds Green
Stonebridge Park and Staples corner.

Take the fast lane to Barnet or Muswell Hill
In a car or a heavy goods vehicle
Get your kicks on the A406.

If you're at the Great Cambridge Interchange
Then Bounds Green and Southgate are in range
Get your kicks on the A406.

If the Lee Valley
Is right up your alley
Or the Woolwich ferry
And the Islington cemetery
Travelling can be drastic
In a single lane of traffic
In Fore street, Hall lane
And the Woodford interchange
Past Gants Hill, Bowes road
All the way to Woodford and Walthamstow.

So get hip to this timely tip
But be prepared it can sometimes be a bitch
To get your kicks on the A406.

(24) Four Candles - 2022 (page 51)

I'd like........

Four bodings (the uneasy ones)
Four mulers (the easy ones)
Four horsemen (preferably of the apocalypse)
Four calling birds (for Christmas)
Four maldehydes (for Grandad - God rest his soul)
Four tunes (good ones please)

Four seables (you said you'd have some in the future)
Four shadows (if there aren't any seables)
Four sights (if there aren't any seables or shadows)
Four woods (not the ones for the back they were rubbish)
Four brydelsens (I made a killing with the last lot)
Four quarters (they come in packs of four)
Four biddens (they're on the top shelf)
Four maltities (legal ones please)
Four midables (large size)
Four fathers (like Grandad)
Four bearers (if you haven't got four fathers)
Four fingers (just by your thumb)
Four casts (I like the all weather ones)
Four fits (for the kids)
Four nicators (for the girlfriend)
Four mations (with shape please)
Four seasons (Valli not Vivaldi)
Four nations (New Zealand not Australia)
Four lorns (I need cheering up)
Four locks (for the hair)
Four syths (like in 'strictly')
Four skins (hard wearing ones)
And I've just remembered Four gets
........And Four candles please - thank you.

The Two Ronnies......'andles for forks' 1976

(25) On The Bench - 2022 (page 52)

On the bench
Is a lonely boy
With no one to dance with on the dance floor
On the bench
Is an elderly Grandad

Left alone to feed the ducks once more
On the bench
Is a reluctant pre teen footballer
Who's been picked for neither team
On the bench
Is a gin soaked loner
Lost in his alcoholic dreams
On the bench
Is a discarded teddy bear
A young child has since outgrown
On the bench
Is a lad living rough
Forced to leave his family home.

Whether self inflicted or an unfortunate event
This is a prayer for everyone left sitting
On the bench.

(26) Faded And Gone - 2022 (page 53)

In my hometown so much is wrong
Shop windows are smashed
Streets full of trash
It's not a place I feel I belong
My town has faded and gone.

My bank is now a hair salon
With an app in a flash
I no longer need cash
I hear they'll return but I don't know where from
My town has faded and gone.

Once we'd go to Woolies to buy the children a treat
Stop in the park to have something to eat.

But now we just wander through litter and gum
Past the Big Issue man
By a coffee shop brand
Shops on the high street just don't belong
My town has faded and gone.

To the lure of Prime we all have succumbed
Their vans trail our streets
Like Uber Eats
There's no value in bricks or a decent income
My town has faded and gone.

We used to buy clothes from the department store
But since online shopping it's not there anymore.

There's nothing to leave to our daughters and sons
Everything's closed
And there's nowhere to go
No final encore or touching swan song
My town has faded and gone.

We'd stop at the bakers to buy currant buns
Then straight home for tea
Just you and me
Now they're delivered before the day has begun
My town has faded and gone.

We used to borrow books from the library
Now we download them to our IPads for free.

This town was a haven for my Dad and my Mum
Now it's devoid

Of the shops they enjoyed
I guess in the end the stock market won
My town has faded and gone.

Sell It Cheap (Goodbye Wilco)

The empty fixtures
And empty shelves
The half price bargains
That just won't sell
The zombie looks
The hopeless eyes
This shop closure
Is no surprise
The graffiti
On the outside walls
The lost custom
And unanswered calls
The vast array
Of empty prongs
Everything must go
But then it's gone.

Flags for sale
From past occasions
In best front line
Selling locations
Lots of stuff
That no one needs
Like bargain lights
And Christmas trees
One more cashier
Will bewail
Another shop

Administration sale
There's nothing left
To do but weep
Pile it high
And sell it cheap.

People And Problems With Technology

(27) Charge (Parts 1 and 2) - 2021 (page 56)

Part 1

Gotta charge up
Gotta charge down
Gotta keep charging
Charging around
Charge my watch
Charge my phone
Gotta get a charger
Mine's at home
Charge on the bus
Charge on the train
Not fully charged
I need charging again
Face the charges
Charge the bill
I'm in charge
Of an imbecile
Free of charge
Or charging out
Charge my car
While out and about
Charging along

Like troops in a battle
Choosing a charger
Android or Apple
Congestion charges
Ready to be paid
And I'm in the charge
Of the light brigade.

Part 2

Kings and Queens
Great dictators
Mobile phones
Defibrillators
Politicians
Electric cars
Neon lights
And rock stars
Heated seating
Powered steering
Devices for
The hard of hearing
Extractor fans
And WiFi routers
Neff ovens
Motor scooters
High speed planes
And battleships
Fat fryers
And computer chips
All these things
Have in common
Something

Not to be forgotten
That each of them
At any hour
Can be victim
To a loss of power.

(28) Interactive Voice Answering Service - 2021 (page 58)

I had a big problem that was making me nervous
So I called up your interactive voice answering service
I heard a polite voice that I thought I could trust
That told me "your call is most important to us"
She gave me some options one to four
I played them twice, then played them once more
None of them matched what was specific to me
So I decided to randomly choose option three
The same polite lady was back to advise
I must now listen to options one to five
None of them covered what was causing me pain
So I decided to listen to them all over again
I worried I'd be dealing with this all by myself
But then fortunately she asked if there was 'anything else'
She said press one for "yes" or two for "no"
So I chose "yes" and we were back where we were a while ago
But this time she had to perform a security check
She asked me to confirm my age, address and sex
My secret word and favourite pet
Which I knew at the time I'd set them
That later on I'd just forget them
The first response I provided was not correct
So she asked me to perform a password reset
She told me politely what she would do next
And to reactivate my account she'd send me a text
I'd just click the link and type in the code

And once it was done, off again we'd go
I did what she asked and my account went live
Then she read out more options; one to five
This time one of them matched my need
So I happily clicked option "two" to proceed
She told me this option was available online
Then abruptly hung up while I was still on the line.

(29) The Wizard Of Truth - 2021 (page 59)

He was the wizard of truth
He had his morning slippers on
Sipping a warm vermouth
All the world at his fingertips
All those levers to pull
All those new opportunities to be cruel
Everything he needed to know
At the touch of his MacBook Pro
He wasn't afraid of the truth
He was the wizard of truth.

What was he going to tweet today?
What did he want to say?
Where was his rain going to fall
And on who's parade?
What was trending, where were the hits?
The run rates and clicks
Taking time to contemplate
The sources of data he would manipulate
The juxtapositions he could conflate
The fakery he could initiate
Lies so sweet they tasted like fruit
Lies so big they needed a roof
He was the vandal of scandal

There was no truth he couldn't handle
It didn't matter who said it
In the end he always got the credit
With an army of private detectives and sleuths
He was the wizard of truth.

He could take anything
Except failure or maybe a joke
He had broad shoulders but he wasn't a big bloke
He always acted like he was above ordinary folk
Who he loved to stir and poke
He was the product of a broken system
And he broke it
He always went for the vein
He didn't sugar coat it
Pumping out the helium of hostility
Then breathing in the oxygen of publicity
Doing a good trade in embarrassment
Stalking and harassment
Offering private patronage
If you were prepared to be patronised
Take the rap and be his fall guy
He didn't care if he was rude and uncouth
He was the wizard of truth.

The greater his truth, the greater his libel
It didn't bother him if his facts weren't reliable
He always said his art was a lie that told a truth
Which he'd pick or choose on the hoof
He wasn't held in great repute
Other than for being a faceless brute
With a big search engine and a browser to boot
In a three piece double breasted suit

Leading his team like a harem of prostitutes
He was always tapping in virally
To a web of painful ironies
He was both charming and offensive
Leading a charm offensive
Persons of influence were initially apprehensive
Until he put their dirty habits on his expenses
And if they ever got miffed
He could always plead the fifth
He played 'I Spy' with the authorities
Who made all his demands a priority
And carried his burden of proof
He was the wizard of truth.

Putting someone on the rack
Was his most delightful aphrodisiac
Then watching their walk of shame
Would turn him on again
And the beauty was.....
When their bucket of troubles reached it's brim
They wouldn't even know it was him
The author of their pain and single point of failure
Directing events from his luxury apartment in Venezuela
Being royally looked after by a corrupt South American
dictator
Where he could exercise the depravities
Stored within the labyrinth of his Freudian cavities
It was open season for his invasive might
Afterall he'd already taken a great big bite
Out of the declaration of human rights
He took all he could take but gave nothing away
And always searching like a bird of prey
For the next victim or catch of the day

Whose pain or scandal would enable him to pay
For another seafood restaurant in Monterey
Or a new apartment in Seville or Granada
It made him feel less persona non grata.

Everything was just a wonderful wonderful lie
Dependent on what his money could buy
It was disturbing and heinous
That he had his digital hand down our pants
And we all loved his stroke of genius
He'd kidnapped our information
He knew where it was stored
While we'd all crossed over the rainbow
And weren't in Kansas anymore
Truth hits everybody he thought
Whether you're old or in your youth
A TV celebrity or a politician in a polling booth
So what if someone loses an eye or a tooth
It's what comes with playing fast and loose
With the wonderful wonderful wizard of truth.

(30) We Have To Watch Something - 2022 (page 62)

We like to watch our neighbours
We've been told to watch our mouths
We could be watching the clock
Or watching birds fly south
Perhaps we'll watch this space
Or maybe watch the skies
There might be somebody watching us
While we're watching paint dry.

We may like watching telly
Or prefer to watch trains

We may like watching people
Or watching falling rain
We could be watching pornography
Or watching what we say
And all along our watchtowers
We know that everyday.....

We have to watch something because we feel so compelled
To watch something, either someone or ourselves
To watch something, whether overtly or by stealth
We have to watch something.

We maybe on a suicide watch
Or watching someone like a hawk
Perhaps we need to watch out
Or just watch where we walk
We could be watching YouTube
Or watching the BBC
Or maybe it's Netflix
Or we're watching ITV.

Are we watching the river flow?
Or just watching our step
Or maybe watching the wheels go round
Or watching the detectives
We might have someone to watch over us
Or we're watching that man
We might own music to watch girls by
Either way we understand....

We have to watch something because we feel so compelled
To watch something, either someone or ourselves
To watch something, whether overtly or by stealth

We have to watch something.

We might be watching calories
We might be watching our weight
We might be watching the market
Or watching exchange rates
We might watch via a PC
Or through a telephoto lens
We might be watching all alone
Or watching with our friends.

We might be watching our manners
Watching our P's and Q's
We might be watching the world go by
While Big Brother is watching you
We've been told to watch the birdie
And to watch your tongue
But is anyone watching the watchers?
Because they're watching everyone.

We have to watch something because we feel so compelled
To watch something, either someone or ourselves
To watch something, whether overtly or by stealth
We have to watch something.

(31) The Best Ghost Version Of You - 2022 (page 64)

I am the best ghost version of you
I shine so brightly while you just make do
I live in your space way up in the sky
On your mobile phone and device hard drive
I'm you but with a permanent smile on my face
I'm you but always residing in a happy place
I'll raise your profile and put you on show

Just keep sharing your happy snaps and videos
And if an illness or a virus gets the better of you
Because you have no firewall and you're not that strong
Then I'll be the best version of you when you've gone.

I am every message you've sent and everything you've shared
You sweat and worry while I parade around without a care
Everyone likes me and provides an affirming thumbs up
I'm permanently confident while you're permanently hung up
I can live forever unchanging and reliant
As long as you leave me password protected and GDPR
compliant
You can rest assured whether you're dead or alive
I'll always be working hard, reflecting your sunny side.

I remember the day you created me
You shared your first beaming selfie
With your friends, work colleagues and family
Since then I've been the treasury for your special memories
But only the ones that you want the world to see
Not those that are plain and desultory
Or are moments of mundane banality
Or when you're sick with fear and anxiety
Or sad, lonely or when you grieve.....
You can take all that shit with you when you leave.

Music And Films

(32) The Sound Of The West Way - 2002 (page 67)

Staccato riffs
Oversized spliffs
Like trousers like brain
Dredd and fame
Stealing pillows from a hotel room
Strutting your stuff on a mic and boom
The sound of the West Way
Still ringing out today
No dark suits like in 1964
The odd bit of time behind a jail door
Never having complete control
But that's the cost of rock and roll
Single, double and triple
Got to throw a stone if you want the pool to ripple
Johnny reggae
Landed in the USA
Beatbox in New York
You could talk the talk
But much harder to walk
White boy rap
But you couldn't always cut the crap
You put the car in the fridge
And the fridge in the car
With one set of drums and three guitars
From Asbury Park to the Brixton Academy
All the way from here to eternity
......"Newsflash
....vacuum cleaner sucks up budgie"
You let that raga drop
You were no CBS prop
All the way to Pearl harbour
Never quite knew what you were after

Free tickets for a free ride
Taking apart the establishment from the inside
You told the truth but you could also lie
Played gigs in the church
But continued to search
No heroin in your brain
Next thing elevator going up again
.....London was calling and some of us wanted to listen.

The Clash - the only band that matters.

(33) My Greatest Hits - 2004 (page 68)

If my life was a series of greatest hits
I'd concentrate upon the bits
That gave me the biggest kicks
By the year or in a mix
For the dedicated fan
I'd include outtakes and a few also rans
An obscure take here, a B side there
Something hard to find and something very rare
And when my finances were less certain
I'd release the remastered 4K deluxe version
Available in download, vinyl and CD
Packed full of blasts from the past and worth every penny.

(34) The Filth And The Fury (1977) - 2005 (page 68)

Hey Ho let's disagree
Over the fading merits of your progressive rock LPs
Three chords, one chorus, two verses
Prime time television curses
Kick in the TV screen
Of this tired regime

Hang Bill Grundy and Benny Hill
Armed with buzzsaw guitars
Which are tuned to kill
A three day week
And 15 minutes of fame
Things would never be the same
Breakdown the borders
Ignore the doctors orders
Never mind the packaging
Here's the real deal
Music for how you feel
The corporations are losing control
It's no longer cool to play the Hollywood bowl
Switchblade, zip parade, spiked and day glo red
Who needs a catwalk wife in their bed?
Frenetic exchange of bodily fluids
Burn a hippy and smack a druid
It's about now and raw emotion
Not Tales from Topographic Oceans
Seek, locate, annihilate
And tell it straight.

(35) We Never Got High - 2019 (page 69)

We got screwed
We were used
We were down on our knees
We said thanks
But to be frank
We had no money
We were burnt in the sun
We scaled up the bang
We got wed
Went to bed

But the phone never rang
It was clear
And a fact
Our songs weren't commercial
We weren't great
A bit fake
And not controvercial
I used you
You used me
We knew that, so what
We wrote stuff
It was duff
We were never that hot
Never high
In the charts
Or high in our room
Never having
The drugs
Our rivals consumed
We were a laugh
We were daft
Never a threat
We got careers
We grew beards
But rarely broke sweat
I could rhyme
You'd keep time
But out of control
You drank too much
Out of touch
Shitfaced in a hole
All that wine
And the smoke

All those flames
That you'd stoke
All our sweat
Still in debt
And we ended up broke
All the gigs round the world
All the boys and the girls
All the chat and the fillers
All the tea and pain killers
You stayed lean
But not clean
Faced with temptation
Lost the race
Had to face
A future state pension
You still
Got around
Like an old circus clown
Shaking fist
Coz you missed
Being talk of the town
Off their list
Always pissed
Staggering out of a club
In despair
Didn't care
You just liked taking drugs.

And when it all hit the ground....
Everything falling down
Gone like a dream
The world's greatest hasbeens.

(36) Can You Hear Me David Jones? - 2020 (page 72)

Can you hear me David Jones?
I wrote a poem for you
About a wide eyed boy from Freecloud
In a jumpsuit and platform shoes.

Even now we can't help staring
At the makeup on your face
Your enigmatic left eye
And stardust animal grace.

Always turning to face the strange
You had us all in a whirl
Constantly making a ch ch ch change
We were never sure if you were a boy or a girl.

When you laid down on your chaise lounge
In a Japanese velvet dress
You were then way beyond "Get it on"
And Glam Rock's recent success.

Whether riding the soul train
With a screwed down hairdo
Or made up like Aladdin Sane
We all wanted to be like you.

What were you, the Invisible Man?
Or the Elephant Man?
Or maybe the Starman?
Or perhaps just the lead singer of Ziggy's band?

You were always such a pretty thing
And like John always dancing

But you never got off on that revolution stuff
Being three parts fiction and one part bluff.

You mixed history and chemistry
With art school hyperbole
You could be something new, old and borrowed
But what you got was no tomorrow.

You once returned as the thin white duke
With your Hitler haircut and Nazi salute
You ended up day after day
Snorting your brain away
What state were you in?
Du warst in Berlin
Playing both the cracked actor and the young American
And putting out the fire with gasoline.

What put you in the oxygen tent?
Was it speed freaking with Iggy Pop?
After so many late night parties
It took something special to make you stop
So high and then so low
But you'd always be a hero...... even just for one day.

One more time to dance the blues
So let's dance again in our red suede shoes
You were a white star
You were a black star
You were a death star
You were the Spider from Mars.

It was 2016 on the 10th Jan

When the sun blasted your shadow
You got strung out in heaven's high
At the end of the freakiest show
Had there been too many quaaludes and red wine
Or just too many songs and lines?

It didn't feel time to break up the band
And it wasn't the kids that killed the man
Your circuit was dead and something was wrong
They'd be no more messing with Major Tom.....

Can you hear me David Jones?
Can you hear me David Jones?

And some years later, whenever time takes another cigarette, it reminds
us you were such a genius and so deserving of that epithet.

(37) Blind Boy Grunt - 2020 (page 74)

I first heard you in my Daddy's car
Sitting alone as he pumped Five Star
You had this voice so thin and lean
It felt so real, you know what I mean.

Blind Boy Grunt
You changed my life
You cut right through me like a carving knife.

You had a way, a way with words
You had the best darn lyrics that I'd ever heard
I played all your records, they were second to none
In the wee small hours before the rising sun.

Blind Boy Grunt
You turned it around
When you played your thin wild mercury sound.

I was the brother that you never knew
While you straddled the world, I was lacing my shoes
The ghost of electricity never howled in my bones
No one called me Judas and I never got stoned.

Blind Boy Grunt
You were a cunning stunt
When your mother nursed the litter I bet you were the runt.

I never had a vision, God didn't speak to me
I didn't sing for Jesus or have an epiphany
I wasn't converted or saw the light
I never had a comeback or a cause I could fight.

Blind Boy Grunt
Laughing on the slow train
Telling the same old joke again and again.

My never ending tour was my journey to work
The one time I protested was over paperwork
I've been doing the same job for thirty six years
No one is going to reappraise my wonderful career.

Blind Boy Grunt
You can be full of crap
That girl drinking champagne should get off your lap.

I read every book they wrote about you

To solve your mystery and unravel your clues
Your prodigious output won't ever cease
I hotly anticipate what you haven't released.

Blind boy grunt
Don't ever stop
Keep on rockin and rolling until you drop

(thank you Bob Dylan)

(38) You'll Never Live Twice - 2020 (page 76)

Surely this world can't be enough?
It's just too rowdy and too rough
There is no man with the golden gun
There is no empire of the sun
It lets us live and lets us die
And all we do is give in and cry
You think it's a wonderful life?
But you'll never live twice.

We're children of the silver screen
Midnight cowboys and closet queens
Prima donnas, sensitive souls
Hoping it's not us for whom the bell tolls
We all use the usual suspects
CGI and special effects
We hide self doubt behind dry ice
Please don't forget you'll never live twice.

Sometimes it's just a bridge too far
We never feel quite like a movie star
We're strangers on the train
Waiting to be entertained

By the next star and by the time they're born
It will be them, not us, the fans will fawn
Our underwhelming paradise just isn't so nice
But we accept it because we'll never live twice.

The empire will always strike back
The mirror will always get cracked
There are too many rebels without a cause
Too many censors with too many rules
So let's check into the priory
With Bridget Jones's diary
And reflect on these words of advice
That you'll never live twice.

There won't be a heavenly sequel
We can't go back in time and create a prequel
Everything is here and now and on general release
Our only guarantee is our runtime will be brief
Critics won't shower us with plaudits
For getting old and falling to bits
There's always one last roll of the dice
But you'll never live twice.

The remains of the day or affairs of our heart
For matinee idols or boring old farts
We'll drift into the shadowlands
Then silence, unless you're a lamb
No more life with psychos in a frenzy
We'll no longer be haunted by greed and envy
Was it worth the ticket price?
Either way you'll never live twice.

(39) Hey Goodbye Warren Zevon - 2021 (page 78)

Hey goodbye Warren Zevon
And your werewolves of London
A story all too familiar
You knew life would kill ya.

You could play it all night long
Lawyers, guns and rock songs
You would stand there in the fire
You had a dirty life and times we all admired.

They called you Mr Bad Example
After a bad luck streak in dancing school
You played Seminole bingo
With a gorilla who was a desperado.

You were headless, reckless and persona non grata
But ended accidentally like a martyr
Never thinking you'd pay so dearly
For boxing too clever with Boom Boom Mancini.

Like Jeannie's shooter you were too easily led
And you wouldn't sleep until you were dead
So you went back to Denver and the high life again
Playing too long in the wind and it's hard steady rain.

Carmelita wouldn't hold you when you told her to shut up
You got all strung out on heroin and now your shit's fucked up
You weren't in the house when the house burned down
But something bad happened to this clown.

You asked for volunteers for your next trick
While striking up the band but then you got sick

Now your ride's here and leaving far too soon I fear
I'll keep you in my heart - you're my mutineer.

(40) Singing The Blues Again And Again - 2021 (page 79)

I woke up this morning saying the same thing twice
I woke up this morning saying the same thing twice
I'm sure I've said this already
I might need some professional advice.

I said Mama listen, I won't say this again
I said Mama listen, I won't say this again
I feel like I just keep repeating myself
It's driving me insane.

The boss said son I've heard this before
The boss said son I've heard this before
Don't tell me it again
I don't want to hear it any more.

I think I've already said this or is this just deja vu?
I think I've already said this or is this just deja vu?
It's the same movie playing
At a cinema near you.

I said hey girl I'm thinking you said this once yourself
I said hey girl I'm thinking you said this once yourself
It still sounds the same to me
I should go talk to somebody else.

I was forced to say it again just for old times sake
I was forced to say it again just for old times sake
Once was enough
Twice is more than I can take.

(41) Cover Of An Old Country Song - 2021 (page 80)

I lied to you
And made you sad
It went on for too long
Now bitter words you sing to me
In a cover of an old country song.

We had it all
We had a ball
We both knew it was wrong
Now the only thing that means anything
Is a cover of an old country song.

I got hooked on gin
And the thrill of sin
Why was this urge so strong?
Now all I do is listen to
A cover of an old country song.

Tonight I'm drinking
In the bar downtown
Until the pain has gone
Those good ol' boys they're playing still
A cover of an old country song.

The lonesome bell
It tolls for me
Telling me to move along
I was never great, just second rate
Like the cover of an old country song

(42) Hey Hey Mama - 2021 (page 81)

I was trampled under foot
I was dazed and confused
I've had good times and bad times
Since I've been loving you.

I need a whole lot of love
And a stairway to heaven
I'm going to California
With a Black Country woman.

Did I fight the battle of Evermore?
And what is and what should never be?
Was this Achilles last stand?
Or just the Houses of the Holy.

Your time is gonna come
You know that's the way
How many more times
Must you miss your celebration day.

It was nobody's fault but mine
To ramble on
I'm gonna bring it on home
After ten years gone.

When the levee breaks
I'll boogie with Stu
On the night flight to Kashmir
Babe I'm gonna leave you.

I will sing my immigrant song
Even though the song remains the same

It will be in my time of dying
When I am sick again.

"To be a Rock, and not to Roll..." — Led Zeppelin

(43) No Mr Bond, I Expect You To Die - 2022 (page 82)

Time flies when you're having fun
But one day you'll have to bite the bullet
My actions will speak louder than your gun
Is that a finger on your trigger, ready to pull it?
I'll pour you one more Vodka Martini
Then consider how I can plot your demise
One more quip and then straighten your tie?
No Mr Bond, I expect you to die.

You know you can't ever kill me
No matter how many times you try
You can't teach an old dog new tricks
And I should let sleeping dogs lie
You appear inevitably like an unloved season
You had your six, now it's my turn I surmise
I take the shot but do you survive?
No Mr Bond, I expect you to die.

Oh not another gun barrel sequence
When you stroll on from stage right
All your Bond girls and decadence
Feel, today, a little overplayed and trite
I guess it's up to me to look after you
Make sure harm doesn't pass you by
Another distraction or one more surprise?
No Mr Bond, I expect you to die.

You're just a kite dancing in a hurricane
Because Mummy has been very bad
And I'm more than a maniacal enemy
Not just deluded, psychotic or mad
I won't be unveiling my plan
To a Cold War pugilistic spy
Will you once more deny me my prize?
No Mr Bond, I expect you to die.

Come come, Mr Bond you disappoint me
But I guess old agents die hard
That last hand nearly killed you
But you still went and played another card
At the drop of a hat you're onto the next spat
Nothing seems to make you give in and cry
Is luck once more on your side?
No Mr Bond, I expect you to die.

(44) Like Karen Carpenter - 2022 (page 83)

It used to feel like they'd only just begun
In the years when they weren't wedded enemies
But today isn't yesterday once more
And every Sha La La brings back painful memories
She didn't feel her age but she was tired
Tired of their tiffs when he would laugh at her
Now for all she knows and it's beginning to show
She'll say goodbye to love like Karen Carpenter.

They used to be on top of the world
Looking down on creation
But now she's left the marital home
With her ticket to ride to a new destination
At first, it felt their hearts might burst

But now passion's pulse never beats faster
She had to choose and not an easy thing to do
And say goodbye to love like Karen Carpenter.

Now there's a kind of hush all over their world
The occupants are silent and there isn't a sound
The King and the Queen are both in pieces
And solitaire's the only game in town
A superstar cast of interplanetary craft
Could not have prevented this matrimonial disaster
But now it's passed and she can leave at last
And say goodbye to love like Karen Carpenter.

To be free of his lies and trickery
There were some tough things she had to do
And in their divorce decree it was agreed
Within a 3 mile radius he'd not 'get close to you'
Keeping up the masquerade but just on Mondays and
rainy days
They were never destined to live happily ever after
And now it's time for her to leave this behind
And say goodbye to love like Karen Carpenter.

(45) Vampires of Venice Beach - 2022 (page 84)

I saw a vampire in the Santa Monica Boulevard
Sipping an iced cold caramel Macchiato
He was wearing a Ted Baker four pocket leather jacket
Dressed up like one of The Sopranos
I saw a vampire hawking fitness subscriptions
For a gym membership campaign
Someone got eviscerated late last night
Vampires of Venice Beach again.

He's a blood sucking fiend
Always up to something obscene
Recently he's been based in Colorado
I wouldn't hang around him Hugh
He'll make a meal out of you
He ate his heart out in Chicago.

I saw Bela Lugosi and Christopher Lee
Meeting the Governor of California
I saw Gary Oldman and Jack Palance
Playing cards with Lon Chaney Junior
I saw a vampire driving down Highway One
In a blood red Coupé De Ville
He'd heard mention of free plasma injections
For the down and out in Beverly Hills
I heard the one about a vampire walking into a bar
And ordering a glass of Pink Champagne
He'd been part of backstreet feud
Where someone's neck got chewed
Vampires of Venice Beach again.

I saw a vampire drinking Pinot Noir
With a crimson lamb moussaka
He sucked a pomegranate
To help cleanse his palette
Planning to take a bite out of Mina Harker
Earlier that night, under strobe lights
He'd been clubbing with Van Helsing
Who's entourage, were having it large
With Vladimir Putin and Boris Yeltsin
They were doing the undead strut, living it up
Because by the morning they'd be melting
So best hide your gear and cover your ears

Venice Beach vampires love the music belting.

I saw a vampire not feeling that fine
Tired of all the years he'd been clocking
He'd been online with Doctor Frankenstein
Who's surcharges were positively shocking
I saw two vampires posing with a coach party of cheerleaders
Their sorority house was rocking
Don't let them take that selfie
You don't want a bat in your belfry
Or a vampire later to come knocking.

"I saw a werewolf drinkin' a piña colada at Trader Vic's
His hair was perfect" Warren Zevon

(46) Take Me To The Pilot Elton John - 2022 (page 86)

I've been running from the Rocket Man
After you told me to burn down the mission
But now your plan's gone wrong
You still expect me to sing your song
That ballad of a well known gun
So simple but now that it's done
The sun will go down on me and you
And we've both seen that movie too
I've crossed a line and now I'm resigned
To sing that border song
Take me to the pilot Elton John.

I used to be hard like crocodile rock
But Mona Lisa reduced me to tears
It left us both saddened and shocked
She was as cold as Christmas in the middle of the year
She lured me into her lion's den like Daniel

She held onto me and turned me like a handle
I just couldn't get her out of my mind
But then we all fall in love sometimes
Soon things began igniting
It was on a Saturday night and made for fighting
She backed off and fled but I lost you instead
I ended up feeling better off dead
And when I found the courage to say sorry
It was the hardest word I'd ever said
I struggled to deal with this rejection
And our tight lipped tumbleweed connection
I realised I could never truly be with you
I guess that's why they call it the blues.

You told me I might get blown away
Like a candle in the wind
When we met a few years later
You couldn't believe I was still standing
You were staying out of town at a Holiday Inn
Spending your nights in a club with Amorena
You told me she moved like a tiny dancer
I wish I could have seen her
You were both holding hands
And swaying to the local DJ playing your song
Take me to the pilot Elton John.

I'd stayed four nights in the Honky Chateau
Saying goodbye to the yellow brick road
I'd spent too long massaging my ego
It left me feeling unworthy and mellow
I was giving serious consideration to my life under this empty sky
Planning how I'd say goodbye
But when you told me to keep up the fight

You saved my life that night
I told you were weird and wonderful
You said it was no sacrifice at all.

I knew then what I needed to do and where to go
You just had to tell me when the whistle blows
Now we're apart, I won't go breaking your heart
And this time it won't be Mona Lisa I choose
Or my past blue moves
When I made a living selling stuffed caribous..

And now I'm on a timeless flight
Only pausing to get as high as a kite
You tell me I'm no better than a honky cat
But I think I'm a whole lot better than that
I know the Rocket Man is on my trail
And there's a rumour Mona Lisa wants to cast another spell
I hear she's planning to return and follow my beaten track
So I'd better get going before the bitch gets back.

I think it's going to be a long, long time
Before I find the right words and lines
But one day I will finish this song
And fly like a skyline pigeon back to where I belong
But until then....
Take me to the pilot Elton John.

(47) It's Music - 2023 (page 88)

It gets me up in the morning
Gets me ready for a fight
Moves my hands and my feet
Gets me spinning on my bike
Breaks my heart

Makes me sweat
Makes me remember
Helps me forget
Any which way you choose it
It's music.

Gives me purpose
And a sense of cool
Rocks like a mother
Kicks like a mule
Gives me rhythm
Until it's late
Helps me dream
And contemplate
Best served with wine or cigarettes
It's music.

Makes me dance
And makes me sing
Makes me do
Just any old thing
It's my first love
And my last
Either from the future
Or the past
If you love the buzz of a guitar lick
It's music.

It can rock
And with style
They call it pop
With a smile
It has no law

And no rules
It can be jazz
Or classical
It can soothe or it can kick
It's music.

It's a suite
It's a song
The food of love
So let's play on
It's got drive
And panache
From Mantovani
To The Clash
Turn it on or just click
It's music.

"To live without my music
Would be impossible to do
In this world of troubles
My music pulls me through"
John Miles

History And Politics

(48) When Tall Buildings Crash - 2001 (page 92)

When tall building crash
It can be heard across the world
By every man and woman
And every boy and girl
It's the headline, the front page
The intrusive news flash
You better be set and ready
When tall buildings crash.

When tall buildings crash
We ask "Who did this then?"
Was it me or was it you?
Or was it us or them?
How should we respond?
Who should we lash?
Better find something to stand under
When tall buildings crash.

When tall buildings crash
I can't say we're surprised
We've seen it all before
Something tumbles and someone dies
Someone leaves a briefcase
Or puts something in the trash
Or someone flies a plane
When tall buildings crash.

When tall building crash
There's always smoke and fire
Heroes and villains
Fake news and liars
Then the reprisals

We'll dance in the ash
Better take your partners
When tall buildings crash.

(49) Boris Yeltsin - 2007-(page 93)

Boris Yeltsin died today
And soon he'll be buried in his grave
First democratic leader of the Soviet State
He could also sing, dance
Conduct and gyrate
Personal foibles all too transparent
A dominant intellect
Not always apparent
He'd stay on the plane
While the dignitaries waited
His democratic plan both cheered and berated
A free market economy
Let loose across the land
No measures of control
Little seemed planned
A widening gap between the poor and the rich
Lined the pockets of new billionaires
Like Roman Abromovich
He came to the aid of the American President
While blowing apart Georgian dissidents
He marched into Chechnya
To face the insurgents
Fully prepared to install a new government
Was it too much wine?
Or an underactive thyroid
That made his expression
So lacking and void
He would stumble and wobble

Flirt and embarrass
Waffle and mumble
Annoy and harass
International entertainment
The Soviet clown
He would cancel arrangements
Let people down
He bestrode a tank
In a manner bizarre
He was always going to be a challenge
For the USSR
He gate crashed the party
Gave Russia a shove....
He was also friends with both Bill Clinton
And Mikhail Gorbachev.

(Enter stage right someone new to put the boot in
Oh no it's Vladimir Putin....bring back Rasputin.....Russia's greatest love
machine)

(50) 2007 (page 94)

Donorgate
Gordon Brown
House prices going down
Nuclear weapons
In Iran
Trying to find
Madeleine McCann
Cash for honours
Tony Blair
English football
In despair
Missing discs

Of children's names
Britney Spears
In rehab again
Winehouse
Self abuse
Katie Holmes
And Tom Cruise
Alistair Darling
Turkey flu
Poor Bernard
Matthews
Money markets
Taking stock
Bankruptcy
At Northern Rock
Jade and Shilpa
Hate each other
Racial scandal
On Big Brother
Wet Summer
For Rhianna
Keeping dry under
Her umbrella
New to LA
Posh and Becks
Billie Piper
Casual sex
Take That
In the charts
The Ugly Betty
Series starts
Hilary Clinton
Campaign trail

Barry George
Out of jail
Serial killers
In the news
Amy Winehouse
Sings the blues
Paris Hilton
Back in jail
Menzies Campbell's
Campaign fails
Princess Di
Wembley gig
Homer Simpson
Spider pig.

(51) Victorian Oblivion (Or Victoria Falls) - 2013 (page 96)

She hears the call of duty
Then feels rising anxiety
She straightens her cotton bonnet
And takes comfort from her piety
They sent her brother to war
In spite of the family's remonstrance
She wished they'd been more important
And not left things to chance
Curse this world so cold and cruel
To stand and watch Victoria fall.

She always felt constrained
By familial jurisdiction
She was well meaning and well mannered
But a walking contradiction
She wiped away a stray tear
Then wrote to the governing board

Who deal with these affairs
And sing "Your country calls"
"Your request will be considered"
But nothing changed at all
Curse this world so cold and cruel
To stand and watch Victoria fall

She would hide inside the vestry
The war was closing in
The shells, the guns, the soldiers
Her brother's suffering
She'd always felt a victim
Not allowed to be ambitious
Squeezed into a cambric bodice
She was well dressed but capricious
The Duke had watched her pensively
Wondering what strings to pull
Welcome her to the officers' tent
And let Victoria fall.

She decided to write to Louise
Her lips the parchment sealed
Conveying a comforting sentiment
To help Louise to heal
Whose Father had been the captain
Of the HMS Victoria
He went down with his crew
In a state of mild euphoria
To this day she still feels bitter
She regrets he ever got on board
Curse this world so cold and cruel
To stand and watch Victoria fall.

Her prescient observations
Had not failed her until now
When the Duke arrived in a jet black fly
Entered with a gentlemanly bow
He had an unhealthy preoccupation
With the size of her stock of gold
He discussed the terms of marriage
Without appearing to be bold
He went by another sobriquet
He'd treat her like a fool
Curse this world so cold and cruel
To stand and watch Victoria fall.

There were many rumours
Louise had wed a Russian spy
Who paraded as a Count at night
But in the days he lived a lie
"Atención a la marche"
He had often warned Louise
"Take heed of what you're doing
And who you aim to please"
Dear reader .....don't be fooled
There's no mystery to enthral
Just words on a world so cold and cruel
That stands and lets Victoria fall.

"Albert" Louise called to the Count
"Get me my smelling salts
In the jewel encrusted casket
That Uncle William bought
I think I have the vapours
Or my corset is too tight
Let's go save some prostitutes

Help them to see the light
Bring them here, for tis my steer
Serve them muffins in the hall"
Curse this world so cold and cruel
To stand and watch Victoria fall.

In a far off sun drenched jungle
In a wild unholy land
Resides a spectacular feature
The empire now commands
Louise has been there once or twice
And I believe so has the Duke
But not Victoria's brother
As there's nothing there to shoot
In a gap within the clearing
Is a wondrous waterfall
Some call it smoke that thunders
And it's where Victoria falls.

(52) Election Time again - 2014 (page 99)

It's time to scrawl that cross again
For someone you don't know
It's time for the swingometer
And the deft touch of Peter Snow
It's time to deal with issues
Run the Mori polls
Unprecedented disasters
Gaffs, hiccups and own goals
The extended edition of question time
To put MPs through their pain
It's time to get on the battle bus
It's election time again.

It's time for manifestos
And time for new campaigns
Let respected gentlemen
Be criticised and defamed
It's time to improve the economy
The state, the health and crime
It's time when opposing parties
Draw up their battle lines
When every Tony, Dave or Maggie
Gets their 5 minutes of fame
We've all got an opinion now
It's election time again.

It's time to use your influence
To be seen and to be heard
It's time for TV satirists
Bremmer, Fortune and Bird
It's time to launch the soundbites
And reputations bury
Time for all the activists
To make the world binary
It's time to find the culprits
And apportion blame
Lets gather round the polling booth
It's election time again.

(53) Constantine - 2014 (page 100)

Rome's global grip was failing
New ways replacing old
But it still held half the world
With the armies it controlled
Barbarians marching from the left
Christians to the right

Rome quelled this resistance
Despite its fading might.

Constantine was troubled
By this possible defeat
His heart scaled to the heavens
When in prayer at Apollo's feet
His family meant more to him
Than flesh and blood and light
He would pay to honour them
And expand their lands and rights.

He led many savage campaigns
To fight the barbarian horde
He never once hesitated
To go to battle when he was called
But he felt an ill wind stirring
He sensed it and he knew
He needed to cut or cauterise
The source from which it grew.

Acclaimed in Eboracum
When engaged in civil war
He was victorious and sole ruler
Of Rome in three two four
He could feel the world a-changin'
The old Gods' rule would cease
So he put and end to paganism
And built a new Rome in the east.

Rome's belief in the sun gods
And Jupiter and Mars
Now had little relevance

There was more meaning in the stars
So he coerced the Roman pagans
To believe in a Christian God
And at the Council of Nicaea
It was approved by its synod.

While marching into battle
At the bridge of Milvian
He saw a cross of light
Held in the palm of God's right hand
He called this cross God's vision
To which all men must pay honour
And the words written in the sky
"Under this sign we conquer".

But did he expect what followed?
So many people slayed
Over every Nicene difference
And misguided crusade
Every weapon of destruction
Or power hungry throne
Can be traced back to this point in time
When these terrible seeds were sown.

A reptile can shed its own skin
Then dine on the remains
But no man should kill another
In defence of God's name
A thousand years and more
Of weak causes and parades
Providing feeble excuses
To pillage and invade.

Oh Constantine your legacy
Is one of terror and affray
Friends, Romans, countrymen
Murdered to this day
Oh Constantine your history
Warns us to beware
For when we look upon your deeds
Even the mighty must despair.

(54) This Is Britain (2016) (page 103)

A tempest just before the dawning of the day
Then after the flood our land's in disarray
From the white cliffs of Dover to the Orkney Isles
A new nation state of distrust, disappointment and denial.

This is Britain
Divided and alone
This is Britain
With no direction home.

The crown of leadership in fear gets passed around
No one keen to wear it while the ship is going down
The poorest judgement since Eden's Suez Canal
A newspaper headline reads "What the hell do we do now"?

This is Britain
All tables overturned
This is Britain
We just might crash and burn.

Our considered diplomacy reduced to a game of thrones
A referendum disinterred and we're picking at the bones
We've been so reckless, so rash and oh so cavalier

We've opened up Pandora's box and let loose the dogs of fear.

This is Britain
Auf Wiedersehen, goodbye
This is Britain
Same arrow, different eye.

Meltdown expected as John Bull closes in
London's calling but the message wears so thin
A sickness in the air carried by a poisoned creed
We saw the warning signs but refused to take any heed.

This is Britain
Reflected in a broken mirror
This is Britain
Wading in a dirty river.

Poorly conceived the wrong question to be asked
How sad to see us move so quickly from fact to farce
The best lack the conviction to speak up and be heard
While the worst...well they're just absurd.

This is Britain
Just blink and it's gone
This is Britain
Too late to right a wrong.

Can you hear the echoes of a bygone civil war
Can you see the ghosts of Edgehill and Marston Moor
Days of political remonstrance and Brittainia's broken rule
The inexorable march to regicide in a January, so cruel.

This is Britain
In a soundbite tit for tat
This is Britain
Charles the 2nd won't be coming back.

The trees bow their branches and the lion sheds a tear
Any strength through unity is at an end I fear
When next we walk again in this new Britain we've created
We'll still be British subjects but divided and isolated.

This is Britain
On the edge of catastrophe
This Britain
Unthread the Bayeux Tapestry

This is Britain
A land once of hope and glory
This is Britain
Now who's sorry.

(55) The Buck Stops - 2017 (page 105)

There's a rumbling in the workplace
There's a fire in the hall
She's trying to ride forward
But her horse is in the stall
A wild storm is brewing
And it's picking up speed
Our blessed country has gone to the dogs
Without any collars or leads.

Everyone is asking
Are we in or are we out?
She might have given us an answer

If she knew how to work it out
You can't roll up an ocean
Or tell the wind when to blow
Let's not carry on pretending
This isn't now a shit show..

She's lost the keys to the shires
And the ears of city gents
Leaving means leaving
But who knows what she meant
We're getting frustrated
Confusion taking root in our heads
So we size up our neighbours
Take it out on them instead.

There's money in the counting house
There are beggars on the make
Concepts of rich and poor
Are starting to break
We have all known hard times
We've all had consequences to face
And yet coherent conversation
Is all over the place.

There are too many cooks
And not enough broth
Too many scissors
And not enough cloth
A bird in the hand
Is worth two in a bush
So why go straight to shove
Before we've even tried to push.

Global integration
We're getting closer by stealth
But some of us still want to
Recreate the commonwealth
I've been roaming up and down
Parliament square
Everything looks up for discussion
Including breathing the air.

We've all taken a stand
There are no exceptions
Even chickens crossing roads
Have their intentions questioned
We have no prenup
We can seek to enforce
And we won't be getting wedding presents
While we're filing for divorce.

(... it's a mucking fuddle)

(56) The Donkeys Are In Charge - 2018 (page 107)

The donkeys are in charge
They gather in their donkey pacts
Discussing their donkey facts
Chewing up the same field
Making no difference to the yield
The donkey self interest
Of different donkey groups
Tails swatting flies
Long faces and sightless eyes
Same old bray
Same old hay

The donkeys are in charge.

The donkeys are in charge
Don't ask them for an opinion
They're only donkeys
They can stamp their hoofs
Trot and stroll
They're weather proof
With nowhere to go
No one leading
Or taking the upper hand
No one donkey
Making a stand
Are you surprised?
The donkeys are in charge.

The donkeys are in charge
It must be really hard
When you're two steps away from the knackers yard
To do the right thing
So they can all move on again
It must be a real strain
When you've got a donkey brain
They just want to stay in their acres
They aren't movers and shakers
They're just so uninspired
And really tired
All they want to do is have a roam
Around their gardens and stately homes
One can only assume
No one's addressing the elephants in the room
Because the donkeys are in charge.

The donkeys are in charge
Oh no not Nigel Farage
Another annoying ass
Let's hope he doesn't last
With his ego bigger than a barge
And a brain nowhere near as large
But larger than one belonging to a donkey
Who's legs are a bit wonky
Singing in the wrong key
Smoking cigars in their donkey jackets
Taking it out on their civil servant lackeys
They won't go far
In their chauffeur driven cars
Unless it's to the abattoir
Oh no, the donkeys are in charge.

(57) Politicising Hope - 2018 (page 109)

Press primed and ready to take a picture
Of him running in Ladbroke Grove
He jogs by a body lying in the high street
He's got a dinner date with the Goves
He's just another political travesty
Sex, shame and favours on the side
He covers up with a shifty apology
Which strongly imply he just lied
He's closing down another unsafe shit tip
A poorly clad mental health ward
Paying off a parliamentary lobby
And another chairman of the board.

They're politicising hope
They're politicising hope
They think that will get our vote.

It's not about a national agony
We think we're better than that
It used to be about slaying dragons
Now it's about herding cats
They think that we're away with fairies
Not united or that great
They say a kingdom is coming
But how long do we have to wait?
She seeks divine intervention
A party member who can save the day
But they're all way beyond redemption
Standing on their feet of clay.

They're politicising hope
They're politicising hope
They think it will help us cope.

Down around the streets of the Embankment
You can't get jack for a deal these days
It's a place where nothing is illegal
There are just different shades of grey
One more reported altercation
Someone else goes under the knife
In A&E they patch the lacerations
And stitch back another life
And so another political shitstorm
An apparatchik tries to clear up the muck
And when it finally goes pear shaped
Blame it all on project cluster fuck.

They're politicising hope
They're politicising hope

Putting us under the microscope.

The press think he's a bit ofa wanker
He's known for always sitting on the fence
He chairs the committee for expansion
He thinks all his constituents are dense
He's got a caricature in the Standard
That looks an awfully lot like him
He'll never be over animated
Being awfully nice but dim
They give him a political sinecure
He gets them a donation from Dad
Who'll get a future investiture
For being an old Etonian Oxbridge gonad.

They're politicising hope
They're politicising hope
Tip toeing across the tightrope.

All the way from Camden market
To the A&E in Northwick Park
Passing by the beggars in the high streets
Sex workers prowling in the dark
Washing cars or delivering parcels
On less than zero hour contracts
Drowning in a sea of administration
Or perpetually being hacked
Never ever finishing anything
Not focussed or feeling well
Riding on a highway to nothing
All resistance shot to hell.

They're politicising hope

They're politicising hope
Sliding down the slippery slope.

(58) Clear Cut - 2020 (page 112)

Sure, tear down another statue if you want to
But please mess with someone else's brain
Are you going to stand there and judge me?
Because I said nothing in support of your cause again.

Because I don't act in a certain way
And I've got no stones to throw
Doesn't mean you can tell me what to say
Or which direction I should go.

Yes I know it's a tragedy
And you want me to make a donation
But if I choose not to do so
Don't accuse me of false allegations.

I've seen you with your spray paint
Read your posts and seen what you wear
But just because I choose not to act the same as you
Doesn't mean that I don't care.

You've got a lot of nerve
To talk about me like you do
You've never seen through my eyes
Never walked a mile in my shoes.

We're living in an age of heartache
Which we're all trying to reverse
We've all got trials and tribulations
Don't make them ten times worse

Yes I'm a child of the sixties
I'm not going to pretend
You say you want a revolution
Well you won't get one this way my friend.

You can't just divide the world
Into terrorists and heroes
We're not simply clans or tribes
With different stripes and hairdos.

The dividing lines you think you see
Are murky, dull and faint
A blend of one part sinner
One part soldier and one part saint
Both Caesar and Gandhi
Went to similar extremes
Castro and Kennedy
Aren't as clear cut as they seem.

(59) Who's Going To Make America Great Again? - 2020 (page 113)

They bomb and invade
With shock and awe
They eavesdrop on conversations
While bending the law
They'll break up families
In the name of democracy
Turn the landscape to flames
Sell tigers to the criminally insane
Tell me who's going to make America great again?

They raise cattle in their prairies
Then kill them by the score

Pack up their meat containers
And import them to our shores
They give us drive-ins that we can be sick in
After eating their chlorinated chicken
Selling us fast food like cocaine
Tell me who's going to make America great again?

They promise peace and prosperity
They have God on their side
As well as the CIA
And the FBI
They'll suck dry and spoil
Any country that can spit out oil
Start the fire then fan the flames
Tell me who's going to make America great again?

They have psychos kill their heroes
They shoot them in the back
Like they did to Abe
Martin, Bobby and Jack
They spend billions on wars they can't win
No matter what the price or suffering
More stars and stripes and pain
Tell me who's going to make America great again?

You could be Sunni or Shiite
Muslim or Jew
Mexican or VC
Either way they'll get to you
You might have a plane or a car
Or a nuclear bomb
Either way they'll have a bigger one.

They are a weapon of mass disruption
They can be ignorant and vain
They've made mistakes
And they've made an art form of repeating them again
They take away freedoms and free will
But not the freedom to shoot and kill
For which they won't ever take the blame
Tell me who's going to make America great again?

They penetrate lands that are holly
They come in hard but then leave slowly
They've got soldiers who blow their top
But follow orders to the fucking full stop
They're so proud of their cowboy manners
And playing the natives the star spangled banner
Then treat them with the utmost disdain
Tell me who's going to make America great again?

"Let's make America great again" Ronald Reagan 1980
"I believe that together we can make America great again,"
Bill Clinton 1992
"Make America great again" Donald Trump 2016.

(60) The Empty Throne And Hollow Crown
-2021 (page 115)

After a hundred years of war
He finally led his men to victory
His enemies were weak
And their armies he repelled.

Sailing across the sea
The last of the Merovingians
His soldiers at his side

The Knights of the San Michel.

No one could distinguish
If he was European or English
He'd been the scourge of Anjou
But also England's greatest fear.

He felt no shame
For all his brutal slaughter
And though without compassion
He was neither reckless nor cavalier.

His cousin bent the knee
Forced into capitulation
Once heir presumptive
Through his dynastic and scheming plans.

Who's own protracted war
One of swords and roses
Had for thirty long years
Raged and weakened his land.

It started years ago
His sister, with child, against his wishes
Who bore a son
Another claimant to the throne.

Under the shadow of night
His guards raided her castle
They said for her child's protection
But they made him captive in her home.

He snatched his sister's land

From England all the way to Aquitaine
Left her destitute
And relying on the kindness of fools.

All the Dukes and Earls
Lords, Knights and noblemen
Gathered in rebellion
Against a ruler weak and cruel.

He was no Curtmantle
Or Coeur de Lion
Not even a Beauclerc
Nor born in Bordeaux.

He was led by his court
Not the will of Parliament
Following only his favourite
He had nowhere else to go.

His darling shone at court
An object of his favour and dalliance
With his ebony eyes
And purple apparel.

Who took his share of land
Titles, duchies and riches
Laughing at the Lords
Who weren't sure if he was a boy or a girl.

Revolution in the air
Plots and whispers
Jealous of his fortune
They'd slay him for his crimes.

Then the madness of the King
Who was mute and unresponsive
His favourite took the crown
In these truly desperate times.

King Death arrived
On ships laden with fineries
Flagons of wine
Soft linen, wool and salt.

On the backs of rats
Rode this fatal miasma
A scourge across nations
No priest or King could halt.

People and plague
In a pot was steaming
Four pence a head
Enforced by brokers and thieves.

The peasants took a stand
Church and state battling for power
In this ungodly hour
No one knew what to believe.

Then the battle on the hill
The path of least resistance
The longbows poised
To rain chaos, havoc and awe.

The forests were burning
As they got into position

They broke his flank
And hammered the favourite to the floor.

The brother took the throne
A move not welcome or expected
Red rubies and ermine
Adorned the crown he'd won.

Each morning at mass
He'd chant from a book of canticles
In prayer and petition
For the Queen to bear a son

Pax Romana was undone
No turning now from his schism
And spurious claim
He was God's right hand.

No saints were marching home
The abbeys deconstructed
The rosaries rejected
But no prince arrived as planned.

They held her down
As the swordsman's blade was sharpened
A hundred days ago
She had been his fairest rose.

Now England was burning
The white falcon had fallen
After supremacy and succession
There was nowhere left to go.

This cycle of rebellion
Driven by people, events and subterfuge
Rising tides of change
As kings and queens move up and down.

They leave their valedictories
We remember their losses and victories
The embers of their legacies
Their empty throne and hollow crown.

"Uneasy lies the head that wears a crown."
William Shakespeare.

(61) This Is My Land - 2021 (page 120)

The gentle undulations
Of my hillsides verdant and hazel
Pregnant with the promise
Of honey dew mornings
And shaded woodlands
Caressed by the sky
And the soft whisper of clouds
Beautiful chaotic
Wild pink woodland cyclamen
Random brushstrokes of green and amber
Splashed across a canvas of scrublands and forests
Lush and fecund
I'm waiting for the buds of spring
The spray of early morning rain
Cooling the embrace of decay and rebirth
Awakened by early morning bird song
This is what I see, this where I stand
This is my land.

Cut to the steely eyes of Kings and Presidents
Eagerly surveying the terra firma of their bordering brothers
Coveting their resources and riches
They are making invasion plans
Marshalling armies
Preparing their emissaries
With new diplomatic pitches
Digging new trenches
Cleaning out the gas masks once again
Starting the long march across cobbled roads and muddy
fields
And no matter how hard we resist
We'll be worn down until we cease to exist
They'll steal every spec of our earth and every grain of sand
This is my land.

Later we'll be car bombing the churches and embassies
Eradicating the invading infidels
Capturing those non believing imbeciles
Cauterising their heresies
Once more in the name of God
And in the name of Allah
In the name of Jesus
Freedom and Valhalla
Take three Hail Marys
And one Hosanna
Start wearing your revolutionary bandanna
Taking apart the political machine
Guillotine the landowners and the ancien régime
It will feel like the worst of times
Not the best of times
Fight for freedom, borders and God's country
Fight foreign invaders and the landed gentry

I've got a knife in my pocket
And a gun in my hand
This is my land.

Years later there will be
Another cheap holiday in other peoples' misery
At the costa del Walt Disney
Anglicise the beaches, make theme parks out of mountain ranges
Jog along to Iberian rages
Pollute the waters put the indigenous population into bars and cages
Let battle commence for the deckchairs facing south
Let pidgin English be the word of mouth
Across the fields and forests we tramp
Turning the world into one big bad holiday camp
This awful raid upon nature's beauty
Just so we can roam free of duty
Turn everything vanilla and bland
This is my land.

How did it come to this? I don't understand
This was not how I planned - my master plan
I look at my works and despair
Scorched earth and exploded rock everywhere
I'm thinking of ending our love affair
You've got a disregard for all that is beautiful and fair
Under the pall of poison you have created
Where everything is driven or air freighted
My disappointment in you can't be overstated
How long do I wait for your ravaging to cease
Or am I waiting for an impossible peace
Take heed and be damned
This is my land.

(62) Silent day, Silent night - 2022 (page 123)

Silent day, silent night
Hide in the dugout and stay out of sight
Cover your ears and hold on tight
Hoping that one day the troubles will cease
And from these burdens we'll find relief.

Silent day, silent night
Pack up your kit bags and get the next flight
Then take up arms and get ready to fight
Load up the guns with ammunition
Dig in for another war of attrition.

Silent day, silent night
Open again the corn beef can
Keep your head down and try not to stand
March with a new expeditionary force
The dead once more will mark your course.

Silent day, silent night
Johnny is getting his gun again
And a Sopwith Camel fighter plane
The day is short but the night is long
No more rolling out the barrel for anyone.

Silent day silent night
We sing of a radiant peace on earth
But the spectre of war haunts every verse
It's blindingly obvious accept to the blind
That the clock keeps on ticking as we run out of time.

Silent day, silent night
Both grab a football and bravely break cover

Kick it around instead of each other
Exchange Christmas gifts and sing carols and songs
Then back to the trenches to put the gas masks on.

Silent day, silent night
Looking back glibly we say it was bananas
That so many died on the field of Flanders
But it's still us old bean, still us old fruit
That reload the mortars for others to shoot.

Silent day, silent night
Paschendale, Ypres, Verdun and the Somme
Kyiv, Kabul, Baghdad and Tehran
To end any war you've got to lose it fast
Let's lose this one together so it doesn't last.

Silent day, silent night
Only you and I hear the screams of fright
Our masks and blindfolds obscure the light
We're born to keep fighting, sadly that much is sure
So I'll fight for my country and you'll fight for yours.

Stille Nacht! Heilige Nacht! - Alles schläft; einsam wacht

(63) His Last Days In Office - 2022 (page 124)

He poured an old Glenfiddich single malt
He'd kept it for a special occasion or calamity
This was definitely one of those he thought
Playing out like a Shakespearean tragedy
But he wasn't Caesar or Henry 5th
And the herd had moved at a very fast rate
Now victim to his own self made political rift
But hey he said "them's the breaks".

He wanted to throttle his enemies
Digging his fingers into the cabinet chair
Knuckles reddening while his nostrils flare
Had they forgotten he'd been London Mayor
But they dragged him kicking and screaming
Across the newly laid rose wood laminate
He'd been royally screwed like a flat pack French dresser
They'd need more than a carpenter to fix this cabinet.

In the end...

It hadn't mattered he'd been a member of the Bullingdon club as an
Oxford graduate
It hadn't mattered his 2012 speeches although vacuous were both funny
and passionate
It hadn't mattered that his deal with Europe had been oven ready
It hadn't mattered it left Northern Ireland both precarious and unsteady
It hadn't mattered that taxpayer money had paid for number ten being
unnecessarily decorated and plastered
It hadn't mattered he'd missed so many fine targets but created so many
fresh disasters.

Because by now he realised that between today and the night he won
There was more to all this than just getting Brexit done,

How had he come to occupy the most senior occupation
With his mixture of hubris and loose political affiliations
Between his periods of inaction and manic inaction
Everything else was smoke, mirrors and distraction
He might have appeared calculating and cynical
But he always stood by two important principles
That the only good laws were the ones you could break

And you could have all you want and still eat your cake.

As they readied the lectern for his valedictory announcement
He was preparing once again to be professionally recalcitrant
He would hide like before in the shadows of the opposition
Be ambiguous about his values and political position
He was empty now, a void in a vacuum surrounded by a vast inertia
He knew for him it was back to the country estate or worse suburbia.

A slip, a handshake, a post and a click
Had resulted in his fall from Gloriana to Tumbledown Dick
Nothing has delivered so little of value or profit
Than the final hours of his last days in office.

(64) The Next Big Thing (page 126)

He's got the hair
He's got the shoes
He's got the riffs
He's got the moves
He's got the walk
He's got the swagger
He's got no money
It doesn't matter
He's got the song you can't help but sing
Put your hands together for the next big thing.

He's got the plan
He's got the suss
He's got more nous
Than the rest of us
He's got the vision
He's got the swing
He doesn't give a damn

About anything
He's always on your phone, making it ping
Put your hands together for the next big thing.

He's got a gun
He's got a bullet
The president's name
Is written on it
He's got no qualms
And no regrets
He's got a face
You can't forget
He was born to cause us pain and suffering
Put your hands together for the next big thing.

He's got the vision
He's got the cause
He's got the team
He's got the balls
He's got the power
He's got the strut
He's got the mouth
He's got the guts
He's heading up a brand new criminal ring
Put your hands together for the next big thing.

He's got the headline
He's got the scandal
There's nothing sordid
He can't handle
He's got wealth
He's got growth
Fame or fortune?

He's got them both
He won't stop until we've crowned him King
Put your hands together for the next big thing.

(65) A British Subject - 2022 (page 128)

The fading of his Master's voice across an empty empire
It's not cricket anymore say the right wing ideologists and umpires
This island life of kings and queens and hereditary perks and power
Now an entertaining rerun of our best days and finest hours
Deluded naval captains still sail the same old shipwrecks
All in all and when it's said and done, it's a British subject.

We still enjoy our foreign affairs and the odd soirée abroad
We can be rebellious one moment then do exactly what we're told
The city of London's drinking cabinets full of whiskies, gins
and tonics
Mid year forecasts, inflation rates and trickle down
economics
Let's keep printing the pound and stamping the cheques
Keep calm, don't panic, you're a British subject.

Half of this fair country is made up of countryside
Full of churches, village greens and tour guides
The rest is a mess of motorways and rusted train lines
Great dirty old rivers and abandoned coal mines
This land is as old as the hills and still uneven and complex
All things considered, it's still a British subject.

Climb to the top of Eton or Harrow on the Hill
Where you can contemplate those lofty spires both tall and surreal
The pillars of a class system that to this day still exists
A breeding ground for Chelsea socialites and young Conservatives
This land is full of head boys, fire marshals and prefects

But at the end of the day it's still a British subject.

Our suboptimal politicians can never seem to quite redeem us
But at least over the years we've been gifted with comedians and musical genius
But we're fundamentally a nation of clerks, cashiers and paper merchants
Car salesmen, dodgy builders, vickers and city gents
We're good at marching, queuing and being present and correct
Keep a stiff upper lip and be a British subject.

We've given the globe the full English, the sandwich and the Sunday roast
Fish and chips, afternoon tea and marmalade on toast
In sixty six we won the cup, an event we still rejoice and clap
Fourteen world cups later and we're still trying to win it back
From Bobby Charlton, to Kevin Keegan and through to Posh and Becks
Football isn't coming home but it will always be a British subject.

We're the patron saint of garden sheds and carpet fitters
Estate agents, mortgages and house price jitters
We're the archbishop of loft conversions and the two bed in the city
Inherited wealth, side extensions and negative equity
Yet there's never enough places to live, buy, sell or let
But any home is a castle for a British subject.

Haha Mr Wilson and oh dear, oh dear Mr Heath
Mr Cameron and Callaghan both reneged on promises and beliefs
Blair and Thatcher have had their day and so has Boris J
And who can forget the debacles of John Major, Gordon Brown and Theresa May
We thought it was in Liz we trust but she's another muppet we suspect
Either way she's likely to be a British subject.

We know it isn't easy and there is no obvious solution
But we can't just rely on days gone by or an industrial
revolution
We've dillied and dallied, lost the van and don't know where to roam
And we can't get tuppence for our old watch chain or find our way back
home
Things aren't great today but not beyond saving just yet
But only if we accept and take a British subject.

Lost Love

(And Lost Lust)

(66) Her Silence - 1984 (page 132)

Her silence
Night falling
Over dust
The blast of cold air
Blowing through the reeds
A cold emptiness
Shrouded by dark clouds
This was a cold place
In a cold peace
During a cold war
On a cold and frozen polar shore
He couldn't avoid this glacial disaster
And she would never have the chance to answer
The question he should have asked her
He heard none of her requests or pleas
She was a cold caller
In this ice age of relentless verbosity.

Her silence
She was lost in a paradigm and couldn't define it
There was no love in this cold climate
The sky was restless
Full of nightmares
And fretful dreaming
He'd left her on the bridge screaming
This is a land of dead wood and dark spires
And bad news from town criers
There's no salvation or recompense
Just icy avoidance and ignorance
And the cold bitter tears

Of her silence.

"*I know a girl from a lonely street*
Cold as ice cream, but still as sweet"
Blondie.

(67) It's Private Practice - 1993 (page 133)

Leather shorts, turquoise hair
Drink in one hand
And a hand down your underwear
Smoky ruin rendezvous
Parquet flooring
Do you or don't you?
Straps of meats
Stitched with hair
Serve it up very rare
Face down upon the mattress
It's private practice.

Weak handshakes
School boy outfits
Cases full of parts and bits
Eyeliner and stencil kits
Be careful where the perfume hits
Upper class misogyny
Rubbing shoulders with androgyny
Amusement parades
Outside arcades
He's a tease, she's an actress
It's private practice.

Window shopping
Low life

Infatuation and inflation
Then all night saturation
Private eyes and private parts
Seedy rooms and tainted hearts
Empty trains
Backseat stains
Freak shows and body blows
Where does all this night life go?
Break that, crack this
It's private practice.

(68) Pulling - 1993 (page 134)

Pulling....apart
Pulling....me down
Pulling....a pint
Pulling....a frown
Pulling....a face
Pulling....a gun
Pulling....a chain
Pulling....a fast one
Pulling....your arm
Pulling....your leg
Pulling....your teeth
Pulling....ahead
Pulling....together
Pulling....it on
Pulling....your hair
Pulling....the other one (it's got bells on)
Pulling....rank
Pulling....into town
Pulling....into a layby
Pulling....around
Pulling....the rope

Pulling....the strings
Pulling....on my conscience
Pulling....on everything
Pulling.....the plug
Pulling.....your weight
Pulling.....up at the rear
Pulling.....out late
Pulling.....up sharp
Pulling.....at my heartstrings
Pulling.....at my heart
Pulling.....someone in the dark
Pulling....all my brain apart!!
All this pulling has got to stop!......it's time to pull my socks up.

(69) Once A Wish - 1994 (page 135)

Once a wish
Twice a kiss
Three times a letter
Four times I met her
Five times at the theatre
Six times she bought me a sweater
Seven times I bought her something better
Eight times I took her to dinner
Nine times tried to woo her
Ten times at the altar
Eleven times a daughter
By the twelfth an affair
And at thirteen she's not there.

(70) Lizzie 1642 - 2010 (page 135)

All attempts at constitutional compromise between King Charles and Parliament broke down early in 1642. Both the King and Parliament raised large armies to gain their way by force of arms. In October, at his temporary base near Shrewsbury, the King decided to march to London in order to force a decisive confrontation with Parliament's main army, commanded by the Earl of Essex.

We feel the pain
Of their cruel stinging rain, Lizzie
They are marching again, Lizzie
With their guns and artillery.

We packed up today
A carriage should be on its way, Lizzie
You know we can't stay, Lizzie
So let's run while we're still free.

You picked a rose
The petals fell upon the road, Lizzie
But the carriage didn't show, Lizzie
I hope they suffer for eternity.

Don't look to me
I can no longer guarantee, Lizzie
We'll live happily, Lizzie
Or evade this misery.

We moved too late
They blocked our escape, Lizzie
They laid all to waste, Lizzie
In their brutal victory.

Raised to the ground
They ruined our hometown, Lizzie
They burnt it down, Lizzie

Now there's nothing left to see.

I march now with the red
But it's to you that I am wed, Lizzie
If I'd stayed instead, Lizzie
You might not have followed me.

I'm overcome
Their web was so well spun, Lizzie
They aimed their guns, Lizzie
Then fired despite your pleas.

I wept and cried
When I heard that you had died, Lizzie
Without you alive, Lizzie
There's nothing left for me.

I'm told feelings pass
As things just never last, Lizzie
But you can't drink from a glass, Lizzie
That's cracked and empty.

I pray at your stone
That one day you'll be home, Lizzie
And I'll no longer be alone, Lizzie
As you're there to greet me.

(71) Enough - 2010 (page 137)

I know you don't want to hear this
I know that it will hurt
I know you don't want to hear this
But hearing nothing is worse
I know you don't want to hear this

But hear what I say, it's true
I know you don't want to hear this
I've heard enough from you.

(72) It's Over - 2010 (page 138)

Over turned
Over looked
Over indulged
Over cooked
Over came
Over come
Over exposed
Over done
Overall
Overbearing
Overrule
Over caring
Over the hill
Over the line
Over the moon
Over time
Over fed
Over subscribed
Over populated
Override
Over me
Overhead
Over you
Over said
Over acted
Overjoyed
Over easy
Over employed

Over sensitive
Over stated
Over the shop
And over rated
Over the top
And over play
Over the wall
And over the hills and far away.

Initially I felt uncomfortable about this poem but I'm getting over it.

(73) A Girl Called Everything - 2011 (page 139)

I wanted Everything
But Everything lived next door
I would have given Everything anything
For Everything's love and more
But Everything is different
Everything is not the same
Everything is beautiful
Everything is driving me insane.

I wanted Everything
But Everything didn't want me
Everything had her reasons
But I had my theory ….(of Everything)
I was told by everybody
That Everything was not ok
Anybody could get hurt
And it could happen any day
I knew Everything had to go
Including her kitchen sink
And anything goes, I suppose
But not with Everything

Now Everything is plain to see
Everything wasn't for me.

I wanted Everything
Everything under the sun
But then she decided to go out with everyone
So Everything came to a head
Because of what Everything did
And what everyone said.

Everything needed something
But that something wasn't me
I just wanted her so much
But I couldn't have Everything.

(As I've got older I can't remember Everything anymore)

(74) You Should Have Stayed With Me - 2015 (page 140)

I don't get how he's still with you
He uses you like a pack of tissues
I think that he's the one with the issues
I wish I could put him in your shoes.

And every night the rain keeps falling
It's true to say his behaviour's appalling.

You should have stayed with me.

I don't know why we've not spoken
It's not me who's feeling so broken
Do you think he's really just joking
You know he's standing there gloating.

Every time he makes a connection
There you are standing to attention.

You should have stayed with me.

He drinks until he's feeling fantastic
Then forgets you're not that elastic
Your actions are increasingly frantic
Are you going to do something drastic?

He has no shame, he's way too cocky
You need to wake up and smell the coffee.

You should have stayed with me

He thinks he's too good to be true
That's why he can keep lying to you
I think you really always knew
He'd turn your whole world black and blue.

You can't build a life while he constantly wrecks it
You need to find a reliable exit.

You should have stayed with me.

(75) Collateral Damage - 2016 (page 141)

I close my eyes and count to ten
I should have called you, instead I called her again
How uncommonly strange and not like me
To act so unpredictably.

She didn't answer, she wasn't there
I left a message for her to hear

Now set in stone, I feel ashamed
There is no way back home again.

I cannot say, I do not know
What this will mean or where it will go
In simple terms, what's done is done
This web of rule has now been spun.

In the dark when I'm in bed
The phantoms of panic fill my head
What will this mean, what should I fear?
What's the damage to what I hold dear?

One minute regret; the next I'm bold
Already the impact starts to unfold
The risks are many and I must act
My natural urge is not to hold back.

So I construct my alibi
But however it's told it's one big lie
Full of loose ends and obvious flaws
It won't hold up in a court of law.

The coffee dregs stare back at me
My bedroom is silent and empty.
The drawn blinds have nothing to say
Accusing eyes won't go away.

I can say now with confidence
All my actions will have a consequence
But to what effect, what dramatic passage?
How many hurt, how much collateral damage?

"The cause is hidden, the result is obvious".
— Ovid, 43 BC-17 AD, Roman poet

(76) I Laid Down-2020 (page 142)

I was laid down on my very first day
When the weather was wet and the sky was grey
The nurse laid me down next to you
I was there from the evening sun to the morning dew
I'd lay down wherever I could
I'd lay awake for hours if I wasn't feeling very good
You laid me down in my first bed
Fears and dreams laid out in my head
And whenever I was suffering and couldn't cope
I laid down.

I was laid up for weeks when I broke my arm
I was laid off school so I didn't come to any harm
I was told to lay on the hospital bed
When you visited and laid your hand on my head
I'd lay down my sword for you in the rain
I'd lay awake just listening to you breathe again
I'd lay down in the cornfields with my friends
And sometimes I'd lie low just to get away from them
And when I felt shy or just wanted to hide
I laid down.

I laid awake just thinking of you
I laid the foundations of a house made for two
I laid his body in the ground
I laid out the plans to turn us around
I laid into you when there wasn't just cause
I laid out my arguments then had to pause
We were laid waste by an infectious disease

We will lay low until it's gone or ceased
I remember our first night under the skylight
I laid down.

(77) I Spoke Too Soon - 2020 (page 144)

I spoke too soon
Before I'd listened
Before I'd learnt
Preferring the sound of my own voice
Too quick to share my opinion
A privilege I hadn't earned
I thought I knew best
I thought I knew what to do
I couldn't see any value listening to you
It would take time, a chore
Anyway I already knew the answer
And it was better than yours
I paid lip service
With a smile and a nod
And when you were getting to your point
I just cut you off
I was so eager to speak
Constructing something clever
I should have paid more attention
But hey whatever
There may have been something in what you said
But too late to know as I just went ahead
And if my ignorance
Comes back to haunt me
My foolishness
Later taunts me
And future circumstance
Rains on my parade

Or bursts my balloon
I might look back and ponder whether
I spoke too soon.

Grow your ears and open your heart.

(78) I Never Meant To Leave You Alone - 2021 (page 145)

I'm so high, up here in the sky
I'm the shadow behind your eyes
I'm in the tears you don't ever cry
I never meant to leave you alone.

I'll haunt you for eternity
But together we will never be
I wish you'd had that last dance with me
I never meant to leave you alone.

> *Fate hangs on certain points in time*
> *That make or break, you know it's true*
> *In that second the grand design*
> *Carves out a place for you.*

You're sitting in your rocking chair
No sign of me anywhere
Life can just be so unfair
I never meant to leave you alone.

They say love isn't universal
And if you lose it there's no reversal
It's in the moment, we don't get a rehearsal
I never meant to leave you alone.

> *We could have been so good together*

The fact we weren't is all on me
In that minute it was now or never
But sadly it was never meant to be.

I had my chance and had my time
But I never intended to be so unkind
There's a love out There we'll never find
I never meant to leave you alone.

(79) Carried You - 2020 (page 146)

I carried you in the wind and the rain
I carried you when you were in pain
I carried you when you hurled abuse in my face
I carried you when you were all over the place
I carried you when you were down on your luck
I carried you when when you got yourself stuck
I carried you when your money ran out
I carried you when you were filled with doubt
I carried you and your bare faced lies
I carried you when you made me cry
I carried you when the trust had gone
I carried you when you were all alone
I carried you and every one of your mistakes
I carried you when you were being fake
I carried you when you said things best left unspoken
I carried you when your heart got broken
I carried you when you were just too heavy
I carried you when you weren't ready
I carried you when you were afraid
I carried you and all of the trouble you made
I carried you when you ransacked my home
I carried you when all you'd do is moan
I carried you when you were laughing at me

I carried you when you were taking every liberty.

Now my back is broken and I'm lying on the floor
I can't carry you anymore.

Reprise
They told me boy you'll carry that weight
Carry that weight a long time
But it's only later I have come to find
That this advice was not unkind
But more accurately a warning sign
Of where I'd need the most help
And it wouldn't be carrying someone else
As the heaviest strain on my mind and health
Is the weight of carrying just myself.

(80) You Gave Me….2022 (page 147)

You gave me religion
You gave me disease
You gave me a partridge in a pear tree
You gave me the answer
You gave me a shove
You gave me a reason
You gave me love
You gave me a wink
Then gave me the flu
So thanks, but I don't want any more from you.

You gave me a fright
You gave me a hand
You gave me things I didn't understand
You gave me a start
You gave me time

You gave me money
You gave me a sign
You gave me a list
Of things to do
So thanks, but I don't want any more from you.

You gave me an order
You gave me a place
You gave me a slap
Across my face
You gave me a seat
You gave an excuse
You gave me a shot
You gave abuse
You gave me opinions
But it was just your view
So thanks, but I don't want any more from you.

You gave me advice
You gave me a scare
You gave me a chance
You gave me a stare
You gave me consent
You gave me permission
You gave me a target
Without ammunition
You gave me a call
Then gave me the blues
So thanks, but I don't want any more from you.

You gave me away
You gave me the creeps
You gave me a send off

It wasn't cheap
You gave me hope
You gave me a ring
You gave me the theory
Of everything
You gave me all this
Then another thing too
So thanks, but I don't want any more from you.

(81) No One Sings A Sad Song Like Joan Armatrading - 2022 (page 149)

Same old tension and dissension
We're running out of reasons to get along
If we wallow in the dirt, no doubt we'll get hurt
How can something that should feel so right feel so wrong
Always stressing, not addressing
The cause and effect of us falling apart
Personal agendas; no surrender
Over time we've anaesthetised our hearts.

We both want to win but it's just pain we're creating
We feel the strain of our resilience breaking
It's a very thin ice over which we are skating
And no one sings a sad song like Joan Armatrading.

Less than zero, we're not heroes
We want to take all we can and never give back
Bitter feelings, aren't appealing
No surprise we get defensive when we feel under attack
We don't agree, obviously
But one good word could cut through it all
One day maybe you'll see what I see
There's more to this than just storming down the hall

We pretend to make up but we know we're both faking
And not soothing hearts that are angry and aching
Or ditching the baggage we keep on collating
And no one sings a sad song like Joan Armatrading,

Masquerading, tears and raging
No one making the first move in our vicious dance
We're out of line, not in time
We refuse to step back whenever the other might advance
We're both to blame and it's a shame
We've drifted up our own self filled creek without a paddle
Inconsequential, not eventful
What's the point of trying to come first in a losing battle?

Some scenes viewers may find upsetting and draining
We're always constantly moaning and complaining
There's no love and affection, a truth we're evading
And no one sings a sad song like Joan Armatrading.

(82) Why Do You Stay Here - 2023 (page 150)

Why do you stay here?
Hiding behind your cloak of disguise
Why do you stay here?
There are lies in your dead water eyes.

I am angry, tired
Disillusioned in you
I see nothing good in pretending
You'll ever be true
But I need you and want you
I worry you won't be around
Am I fooling myself

Will it all just bring me down?

Why do you stay here?
I know you're my great pretender
Why do you stay here?
With a secret and silent agenda.

Inside I'm just crying
But you only see my affable face
It feels like we're dying
I might look fine but I'm all over the place.

Why do you stay here?
You bring nothing and you've nothing to give
Why do you stay here?
If there's love then you keep it well hid.

I'm nervous
Apprehensive
Worried what I will do
If you leave me
I don't know how
I can continue
I'm lost
And I'm losing
Nothing is clear anymore
I try to talk about it
But my nerves are too raw.

So why do you stay here?
When you've got nothing new to say
Why do you stay here?
It would be kinder if you just go away.

There's a truth we're avoiding
We're idiots and we haven't a clue
I prefer things left uncertain
Than know for sure I'm going to lose you.

Why do you stay here?
When you know it's all just in vain
Why do you stay here?
When you know that nothing will change.

Uncertainty And Fear

(83) Protest Song -1986 (page 154)

It has been said in many places
That we should not think less of different faces
And people that are under fed
Should not have to sit in queues and beg
These noble voices from tender places
Who scream at society's disgraces
In their polka dots and Armani glasses
From the confines of their evening classes
We all know what's wrong so where is our protest song?

We hear it in the staff canteen
Behind the bars, in the latrines
The best direction for me and you
By people who know less than they think they do
Pointing fingers, having laughs, between crisps and pints and pints and halves
All the experts of our age
Fumble in communal rage
We all know what's wrong so where is our protest song?

Our papers, cameras and telephones
Encroaching on our private zones
To make sure we're fully aware
Of what's really good and bad out there
We'll know who to accuse and shame
And if we're wrong we'll name again
We'll always know which side to stay
It'll be front page news and clear as day
We all know what's wrong so where is our protest song?

36 years later....2022

We thought we'd seen the end of genocide

154

And the politics of fratricide
No more groups of illuminatis
Preparing to bring back the National Socialist party
We thought our non aggression pacts would hold
And the millennial autocrats could be controlled
And in this 21st century new order
We'd learnt to respect our freedoms and borders
So how did things get to be so wrong?
I really need a protest song.

The next seven poems hang together (loosely) as a poetic suite - a study of the Freudian caverns of fear and isolation through a surrealistic prism (or something like that).

Sensory Deprivation Suite

(84) Missing (In Four Acts) - 2006 (page 156)

She was missing when I got home.

Act 1 - The troubling dream - last night....
>   I woke from a dream all alone
>   With my troubled mind and heart
>   For reasons to me that were unknown
>   So I worried alone in the dark

Was there something I'd overlooked?
>   In my dream....
>   I'd stood at the top of the stairs
>   And you were calling
>   But you weren't there
>   And I was falling
>   Not reaching the bottom
>   I just kept falling

Was there something I'd mislaid?
>   I could see and I could hear but....
>   I could not move
>   I'd lost the power to choose
>   Or decide what was dream or true
>   And I could not wake
>   And I could not move

Was it something I'd misplaced?
>   Perhaps I was fussing over nothing
>   But I sure felt I was missing something.

Act 2 - The dawning anxiety - the morning after the night before.....
>   Did I leave the heater on?
>   Is the flame retardant sofa combusting?

Did I shut the garage door?
Am I lacking confidence?
Or am I too trusting?

That twinge in my chest
Muscular or cardial?
Quick I might need to confess
Get me a priest, where's the cardinal?

Act 3 - The confession- in conversation with a counsellor that afternoon

...

...yes interesting question
....my first memory is of my Mother's sewing box
It was wicker and had tiny little locks...

Hang on .... THIS IS REALLY HAPPENING...............

I don't think I'm crazy
But it's beginning to feel like a scene from
Rosemary's Baby
I'm seeing the sharp point of a needle ready to burst my skin
I see a death mask drawn over a rictus grin
I think I'm due an operation, when will it be
happening?
What about the open bathroom window?
Or the Gideon Bible kept under my pillow?
I can hear the alarm ringing
My phone pinging
The notifications singing
And smell the gas pipes leaking
Everything's short circuiting
And the broadband isn't working
The ceiling is breaking

My roof is cracking and the boiler is overheating
...and what about all the poisons I'm eating
I think I might be in some kind of trouble
I'd know what it was.......
If I could find the missing piece of the puzzle.

Act 4 - The harsh reality - at night after work ......

There was a rumour apparently
In the whispering gallery
Would fear turn to reality?
It's no surprise I feel so panicky
In a world predicated on chaos, self interest and anarchy
I try and make sense of all these disturbing patterns
Perhaps the worst thing in the world just might have happened.

She was missing when I got home
Real life came crashing in.

(85) Not All Together Now - 2007 (page 158)

Static electricity
Hairs standing on end
Clouds casting shadows
From a giant distant sun
Which just got a bit closer
To everyone
Anxious furtive glances
New moves to new dances
There's thunder in the air
A heavy loaded sky
Begins its slow descent
Whispers in corridors
Bad news constantly
Grave predictions on TV

Disconnected frequencies
Trains not running on time
No one working overtime
Random political statements
Blind mutineers
Fools elected to lead
Unilateral ambitions
Political cataracts
Random acts of destruction
Empty churches
Graffiti causes
Pregnant pauses
Exchange rate mechanisms
The rise of populism
New winners and losers
New leaders and followers
New sensations and stars
New music for new charts
Strange behaviours
Uncertain consequence
Unfortunate coincidence
Irrational decisions
Leaving the beaten path
Old alliances broken
Trusted antique furniture
Sent to the scrapyard
Making way for the superficial
And pretentious
Waving goodbye
To the liberal consensus
Old rules cease to apply
In this new modus operandi
Plumes of smoke

Carried higher
From a funeral pyre
Or forest fire
Reheating the Cold War
Burning the grain stores
Old tensions get a restart
The gap between the haves
And those that don't have it
Between money and absence of money
Between the beautiful
And the ordinary
Between the top rung of the ladder
And those who can't even see the ladder
The gap between the north and the south
The east and the west
The self venting old
And the cavalier young
Values devalued
Bad jokes gain status
While dark comedy
Continues to bait us
Nothing smelling of roses
Fake news and poses
We're more angry about less
And less accepting of more
We have strong opinions
Yet we feel so unsure
Action turns to farce
Accidental heroism
Disorder's new order
The resurrection of old borders
Drawn between
Our hygienic regimes

With new ways to stay clean
New ways to express opinions
New ways to be mean
New statements of intent
New pills and tablets
And new commandments
More cardboard boxes
More paradoxes
To preach is to patronise
To teach is to terrorise
To instruct is to wound
To protect is to harm
To love is to lie
The system is broken
But the parts are still moving
But not all together now.

(86) A Nightmare In London (In Four Parts)- 2008 (page 161)

Part 1-that evening-London-Leicester Square…..
Last night in London a movie pixelated into a digital glare
Treating a paying audience to a mind numbing nightmare
One of its stars had arrived earlier in his premiere suit
With members of the paparazzi ready to point and shoot.

This city locks away both the unreasonable and the good
Many would leave tomorrow if they only could
There goes another free newspaper getting blown across the road
It was raining hard and the blocked drains still overflowed.

Part 2 -in a glass fronted Italian restaurant off Wardour Street……
An inherent psychotic cruelty sweated in his brain
He had an unsound desire to inflict humiliating pain
Defame without a consequence, shoot from the hip

Find another face to terrorise or another jacket to rip.

She peered over her glass at his unbecoming frame
He felt her disapproval and she felt the weight of his disdain
They deserved each other and the comments they shared
And the foolhardy notion they might just once have cared.

Part 3-on the 10 o'clock news at home…..
There's always someone fighting; there's always someone at war
There's always a good reason for settling a score
For body count, read massacre in the name of free speech
As we fight insurgents in some off the globe outreach.

The world is getting smaller and everything's closing in
So we take up arms together and bang that drum of tin
John Brown's body was broken in a ricochet
One more war torn paraplegic on one more worthless day.

Part 4-staring into a bathroom mirror….
Perhaps the tears we shed and the occasional loving kiss
Are a hopeful reminder there's a better place than this
Not one trapped between our fears and the fairground
Or chained to a ferris wheel going up and going down
We sense in our hearts things are far from ideal
And it's more than just feeling temporarily unfulfilled
We remember how wonderful it was once to be young
When we were free, feeling at ease and sung at the top of our lungs
A time of dandelions, daisy chains, nettles, leaves and sticks
A time when there weren't any problems so big we couldn't fix.

□□□⊛□□□□□

(87) ......And Another Thing - 2015 (page 163)

He listens
To the backstreet reverie
Full of insincere discontent
He wants to rage against this fabrication
He wants to tell them what he meant
He's been pummelled before
So he can take a beating again
Firming up the muscles in his jaw
But he can't even muster a yawn.

Here he is
Not quite himself
A tiny blemish on a perfect world
Here they are, not quite right
Shouting match restored
.....and another thing.

The Catholics and the bulky boys
Looking to crowbar disbelief
Sarcastic ineptitude
A cycle of tedious motifs
You and those vandals at the wine bar
Comparing stories and wounds
You bragged you were caught and put on the rack
Your brain was scrambled and left there to fry
This premature car crash of a digital savage
With broken toys, gossip and brain damage.

Here they are
Not quite right
They can't remember what you did last night
Here you are
What's your name?
Have we finished now...?

Oh no there's....
.....another thing.

No holding hands or loving banter
He hates the things she just assumes
She makes another cynical confession
In her Big Brother diary room
She's lying in bed with a screwdriver to her head
She tearfully recounts she nearly ended up dead
She celebrates this event via touch screen glass
Let's everyone know he'd been a pain in the arse
She blogs, meanders, shares and tweets
Gathers up her pack and listens to the bleats.

Here she is
Quite absurd
Just like one of those Angry Birds
Here he is
Down on his knees
Feeling ill at ease
......and another thing.

Pushing past old people and Mums with kids
Desperate to avoid that seat facing north
Don't try and catch his eye
There's no warmth there or remorse
The bear market crashed today
The FTSE and the Dow locking horns
He knows the devil's in the detail and his money's in a pit
His fleece is shorn and the safe is blown
He's a man of influence that can't afford a home.

Here he is
Nearly broke
Feeling kind of tender
From the moment he awoke

Here they are
Taking their cues
Get ready to schmooze
....and another thing.

Her biopsy results arrived today
Not great but not terrible
Those therapy sessions hadn't helped
But the Benzedrine made it bearable
That rash on her body and her swollen foot
Don't patronise and tell her it's all good
She's in a red veined panic under a blood red moon
One more stupid thing will ignite her short fuse
Put the fire in her stomach and the smoke in her brain
Will she ever have the power to make choices again?

Here she is
Not quite herself
She knows she's different
But more than she believed
Here I am
Not quite you
You're waiting for something
And I'm waiting to say
....another thing.

The next big thing?
.......political, malicious, social, financial or medicinal ....
Or just another thing.

(88) Oblivion.com -2016 (page 165)

They're opening the windows
The peepshow is for free
As Lady Godiva's chambermaid

Dances in her lingerie
She's on from night till morning
Without fear of penalty
Sharing endless chatter
And soft porn banality
Endless pages swiped
As the PC gently hums
You can always find some comfort.......
On Oblivion.Com.

A wayward armadillo
Posts Florence Nightingale
Has tried to cross the border
Via a South American jail
She cries this is a calamity
And shows why society's broke
It'll end up on some mantelpiece
Or lining someone's coat
She's hoping this will demonstrate
How saintly she's become
Preaching to the multitude.....
On Oblivion.Com.

The feudal lord of New York
Tweeting in his fortress high
Taking lambs to the slaughter
Kissing girls to make them cry
He's a friend of George the Conqueror
Who's Boston reverie
Recruited salt washed sailors
To march on Tennessee
They never got too far
In fact the mission bombed

Now they're writing articles……
On Oblivion.Com.

The messages are descending
And scatter across the land
Leaving words and rumours
That get blown around like sand
Except Disraeli's scandal
Carried on the piper's toot
About the avocado
He shared with a prostitute
We don't know how it started
Or where the news came from
And there is no start or finish……
On Oblivion.Com.

"Look at me" types Alice
"Look how gorgeous I've become
By taking all my orange pills
With Diet Coke and rum
My life is simply perfect
Here's the evidence if you want
My smiley face and hourly posts
In my favourite Disney font
For me there's never sadness
Life Tik Toks along
Apart from what I'm posting…..
On Oblivion.Com".

The journalists are sniffing
There's gossip they can smell
Waiting to print at midnight
Every defect they can sell

The needy and the spiteful
Then arrive on a painted wagon
They've come to suck the nipple
Of the social network dragon
The beaten and the bullied
Seek shelter from this throng
They run and take their cover.....
On Oblivion.Com.

The prince of Transylvania
Had been at it once again
Incriminating online evidence
That he'd struggle to explain
He made a call to New York
To his friend the feudal lord
Whose many hats of influence
Any rabbit could be pulled
He needed it redacted
All traces of it gone
But nothing is ever airbrushed....
On Oblivion.Com.

In Belgravia the princess dances
With a circus travelling man
He's hirsute dark and confident
But a stranger to these lands
The queen is not so happy
Mixed blood will spoil her kind
She then rewrites the statute book
Now it's become a crime
There were rumours of conspiracy
But no one knows where from
Better start up the search engine....

On Oblivion.Com.

He was preaching at the Temple
His crowd were really mad
Neo Fascist morons
Shouting "Ban the Jab"
Up Pennsylvania avenue
Together they would run
Screaming at the cameras
"Which side are you on?"
This anxiety society
Wants you to join their throng
Best to check them out first...
On Oblivion.Com.

Now these words came to me naturally
And I've written them just for you
But the rhythm I have stolen
And all the ideas too
I'm not asking you to like them
Or with other friends share
And if you have an opinion
Well really I don't care
If you're waiting for a sequel
Then I wouldn't wait too long
Unless of course you're surfing....
On Oblivion.Com.

"Right now I can't read too good
Don't send me no more letters no
Not unless you mail them
From Desolation Row" Bob Dylan 1965

(89) Paradise:Copied/Pasted/And Lost (In Five Parts) 2018 (page 170)

1. Logged On

A bad body image and a split condom
The ballistic tests of Kim Jong-un
Facebook delinquents, paradise undone
Theological weapons, shared or sold on
On eBay,Etsy or Amazon
Belligerent conduct, the emperor's clothes
Dysfunctional click, disproportional pose
Rage and simpering hyperbole
Smart or ignorant and down on your knees
Earning a degree or marketing diploma
To cover up the blind spots and scotomas
Nuclear missiles, cruise and coach tours
The daily interest of Love Island viewers
Tea time terrorists, lunch time lies
Hackers and slackers, vigilantes and spies
Wires and liars, snitches and traitors
Kings and queens and great dictators
Sound bites, punchlines, fake news and suffering
What the hell's wrong, the signal keeps buffering
Who'll blink first which supremo is bluffing?
Which lines will they remember? Which lines are they
fluffing?

......and someone screams 'THAT'S ENOUGH'!
No more scorching the earth
Chewing the bone
Choking on smoke
Smoking the toke

Or taking the biscuit
But who's going to stand up and risk it?

2. Password Reset
There I was in a balmy sickly Summer haze
Trying to guide the oncoming tide
Into gullies of sand
Dismembered saltwater crabs captured in my can
The smell of vanilla, vinegar and Ambre Solaire
Fuzzy, hazy, crazy and ill - a queasy dream
Flashing lights crisscrossing and shimmering
Like the start of a migraine or the end of a nightmare.

3. Reporting A Problem
We won't go forward
We won't go back
We're staying right here
What d'ya think of that?

And repeat....

4. Status Update
- The rise of mass digital disinformation in tandem with the breakdown of western constructs has prompted the era of paradox; contradictory positions can now comfortably live hand in hand:
    - We have access to more information than ever before and yet know less.
    - Our problems today are more serious and yet our reaction is erratic, bordering on irresponsible.
    - Our challenges today are more complex and yet we address them with simple childlike sentiment.

- We seek shelter from nuance and ambiguity under banal overworked platitudes.
- Fear is simplified and we simplify our enemies too.
- We have created the conditions for a new type of leader; one who can pander to extremism and couch complex policy in nursery rhyme.
- Who can fulfil the needs of the alienated but opinionated masses.

They will invest in air conditioning while the world warms up.

5. Access Denied

Hopes, dreams, and fears of coming to harm
Now rivers of binary ones and zeros
Stored on hard drives and server farms
And run by big tech CEOs
Everything now is in the hands of the few
Everything under one roof
For a greater degree of efficiency
And the economic management of the truth
Streams of tiny dots and pixels
A tsunami of algorithms and stats
There's no need to engage brain
Just sit back and relax
You might even find what you're searching for, perhaps
But the more important truth, on reflection
All of us now are struggling to find a connection...

- No time to remember
- Nothing to forget
- No need to think
- Nothing to regret.

(90) ….Well Done - 2018 (page 173)

Tramlines, motorways
And hairpins
Sacrilegious nonsense
Overtures and dramas
Painkillers and opera
Trampolines and targets
Disappointing headlines
Lost without directions
Can't avoid the fault lines.

Well done
But out of zone
Like an unsupported mobile phone
Out of reach and all alone
I'm well done.

Dust banks full of useless garbage
Most of it is plastic
The situation's drastic
We're just so orgiastic
I step onto the pavement
Don't look at me that way
Stare at redundant windows
Impotent and empty
Like a discarded trolley
Just another one of many.

Well done
And out of time
Left hanging on the line
Out of reach and left behind
I'm well done.

Fingers crooked and aching
From buttons they've been pressing
Touchscreen and dependent
On messages in free fall
Vacant and delinquent
A ring tone keeps on playing
Not hearing what you're saying
Not picking up on signals
Or the warnings you're relaying.

Well done
You've run aground
Stuck in the lost and found
Atomically quite unsound
I'm well done.

Data
Cyber interruptions
Firewall and viral
Lost in crypto spiral
Facile independence
On the road to nothing
Hoping there is something
Clinging onto punch lines
Simplified religion
Divided into regions
Loyalty and legion
And other tribal stances
Learning brand new dances
And other useless things.

Well done

And all alone
Left to simmer
And can't call home
Now boiled to the bone
I'm well done.

Sensory Deprivation Suite is over .... now back to life and back to reality.

(91) A Fear Of Magpies - 2018 (page 175)

There are magpies in the garden
The other birds have shied away
They are hiding in the treetops
As my alarm clock starts another day.

....later the kettle whistles and I burn my toast
And I've run out of coffee; Waitrose instant aromatic roast
After all this time
There are things I still can't get right
Like replacing the bulb in the upstairs light
I'm on my own
From the moment I arose.
I furtively leave my home
Into early morning shadows
A nervous glance here
I watch my step there
I'm anxiously looking everywhere
But mostly I'm looking down
Eyes focused firmly on the ground.

My train was late again on arrival

In a carriage a moth fights for survival
I try and avoid a group of last night's work men
I hope I don't bump into them again
They smell of Red Bull and fast food
They're loud, offensive and rude.

A garbled tannoy then the threat of delay
I panic that I'll not get into work today
I've inherited all my Father's bad habits
With a few extras thrown in
Like fearing the worst and constantly worrying
I abhor the uncertainty
Of what lurks behind the sliding doors
I ponder what's in store for me
There's so little reliably safe and sure
So I keep my eyes fixed to the floor.

I don't want to give up my chair or my phone
I don't want them to take the keys to my home
There are predators planning to do their best
To kick us out of our family homes and nests
A TFL poster reads "See it, say it, sorted"
That's all very well, but what will they do about the thugs who've just
boarded?
I feel so ill at ease
I wish you'd all stop threatening me please.

The magpie chant goes round in my brain
I can hear it going around again.....
One for the cutter
Two for the blade
Three for praying
Four to be safe

Five for my silver
Six for my gold
Seven for the psycho out on parole
Magpie.

(92) Turbulence - 2018 (page 177)

I was born among the storm clouds at a quarter to four
My Mother hadn't a cot so I slept in a drawer
My Father was still flying home and without an ETA
A man of best intentions until the weather got in the way.

Turbulence
It's getting harder to use the flight console
Turbulence
High up in the sky where the wild winds unfold.

I used to think just flying low would positively impact
What the forecast had in store for me but listen here's a fact
I've come to the conclusion that none of us just glide
Get ready, hold the hand rails and enjoy the ride.

Turbulence
All we ever want to do is just travel straight
Turbulence
Another bout is on its way and I can't wait.

It's more squally than it's ever been, then calmer the next day
Memories of bad journeys never blur or fade away
We can no longer trust our pilot as he's not always in control
Heavy clouds approaching as the plane begins to roll.

Turbulence
Are we nearer to our Gods up here?

Turbulence
Will the shaking ever stop and when will they appear?

We're distracted by the weather whenever it takes a turn
The sound of rolling thunder is always a concern
Hold on to the armrest, keep your feet under the chair
Brace yourself for impact; you're not going anywhere.

Turbulence
Points on our journey when things don't go so well
Turbulence
Anyone's trip to somewhere can be blown to hell.

Brothers, mothers and sisters struggling with the safety catch
Wives, husbands and their children running for the exit hatch
We hope that our allocated pilot is both wise and divine
That there really is someone sensible behind the grand design.

Turbulence
Give it up for all the Hitlers, Francos, Trumps and Caesars
Turbulence
And for any other troubled and turbulent leaders.

High up here things feel always dangerous and threatening
How are we expected to trust and feel reassured about anything?
Accidents do happen but no one knows exactly why
Look, another plane crash in a dark foreboding sky.

Turbulence
Trying to act reasonably on an unreasonable planet
Turbulence
Keep calm, carry on and try not to panic
Turbulence.

turbulence
/ˈtɜːbjʊləns/
violent or unsteady movement of air or water, or of some other fluid.
a state of conflict or confusion.

(93) News Just In…..(Salt Water) - 2019 (page 179)

Too late, much too late
The obituary, the tributes and platitudes
The river will find its way
People are people
But you still were taken away
Your labours and goals
Your friendships and laughs
You posing with your family, mortar board and scarf
Feeling so proud
But then you were in the wrong place at the wrong time...
The commentary in the evening press
The photos, the kind words and quotes
The performers await their cues; their parts to play
Who's going to wipe this salt water away?

Well meaning but do we mean what we say?
Too easy to make a promise in the heat of the hurting
Another city gathering and silenced by the clock
News print over our fingers
Breaking news on our phones
One click away from real broken bones
Overwhelming, overflowing
Red eyes and soliloquies
Displays of solidarity
Together by the marble pillars
Pledges to stick together

And not let this happen again
But here we are; another bad day
Who's going to wipe this salt water away?

Later that week.

Send...
Well used sets of poorly thought out assumptions
Unproven untested textbook consultant bullshit
The fog of well meaning inertia
That turns the harsh realities into snappy corporate sound bites.

Send....
From the blue sky, from the flip chart
From the trays of processors, organisers, developers and other nebulous professionals
New policies, protocols and guidelines; the balm to our self doubts and vacillation.

So one more bland communique
Or screaming headline in the news today
We're happiest leaving things grey
And as a result real action delay
We can't seem to convey our dismay
Or say this is not ok
So our tears on each tragic and painful day
In increments heavier weigh
Who's going to wipe this salt water away?

(94) Going For A Song - 2019 (page 180)

Bent out, feel the pliers
Trapped with the boy next door
Air con in the hybrid

Feel those engines roar
Translate save the planet
Clockface, your time is up
There goes another koala
Under a fire truck.

Vaccination
No need for doctors anymore
Immigration
We're going to shut our border's door
Malnutrition
Elegantly wasted
Capitulation
Accept or face it.

Good deed, daft emoji
A Manga refugee
Submit, face the music
Digital heresy
Let's chat pet insurance
Tax cut, but not for free
Campaign, rock the planet
Burn down the money tree.

Manipulation
Tell me when I'm right and wrong
One nation
We're all going for a song
Saturation
Mass market, packaged sent to you
Population
There's only so many silver spoons.

Hair loss feeling frantic
Chat show reality
Back door, push the margin
Basement banality
"Just eat" is on the menu
Car bomb an enemy
Walk tall, not civilian
Soft top democracy.

Chlorination
You'll have to eat that chicken raw
Repatriation
Invite the neighbours round once more
Inspiration
The beads of sweat on my forehead
Perspiration
Wish to God I'd stayed in bed.

(95) Sonnet - Let's Get Uncomfortable - 2020 (page 182)

I didn't have a problem until you told me I had
Now everytime I look at you, I feel so bad
I focus on the things you told me not to feel or say
I'm conscious of looking at you in a certain way
I want to do the right thing by you, but I thought I was before?
Now I think about the wrong thing and not the right thing anymore
Should I have smiled that way, should I have offered you a chair?
Should I have told you that story, I didn't mean to stare
Do you want me to say sorry, should I offer you a drink?
It's so hard for me to control how I feel and think?
I'll try not to dwell on your different gender, skin and shape
I'll ignore the things that you and I both can't escape.

I'm working on all my flaws and imperfections
Getting myself ready for your next review and inspection
I'll try not to do the things you tell me are so uncool
If you could make me feel a little less uncomfortable.

(96) Displaced -2021 (page 183)

From the back room to the porch
Dying in the living room
As the sun cut through the curtains
Turning the dust into sparks
She turned in her chair
Hands held in prayer
Wracked by spontaneous crying
And her splintering indifference
To the world outside.

Displaced
There's always something on her mind
Displaced
She's not there all the time.

He came all the way from Tiger Bay
With a rucksack on his back
He thanked God he'd got away
From his domestic cabaret
He wanted to be Morissey
Or another rock celebrity
But he looked more like Jesus
In an overcoat and sneakers
To gain some respect
He could be nasty and direct

We wasn't great at following leaders
Or trying to stay cleaner
Between medical procedures
And now he had trouble holding it together between seizures.

Displaced
He's not sure how to cope
Displaced
He used to be full of hope.

She's been too long in the shower
Nearly over an hour
It's the only space
Where she feels warm and safe
She tried to speak about her feelings
But she felt nobody was listening
Between the pauses and the fights
During the mornings and nights
Her car is parked outside
She'd plan to stay a night
No one's died
But she still feels like she's grieving
There's nothing here worth retrieving
She really should be leaving
The water's cold, she's freezing
She just wants something to believe in.

Displaced
She keeps crashing on the floor
Displaced
She can't crash anymore.

In this place

We cry for help but no one hears
In this place
You can fade away and disappear
In this place
We always sleep in and get up late
In this place
There are no lucky breaks
In this place
You can lose all sense of time
In this place
Not much scans or rhymes.

He was staring at the bottom
Of another half empty bottle
Something cheap and bitter
That he'd rescued from the litter
His face felt like leather
He wished he could get his shit together
He was staring into space
While nextdoor's drum and bass
Kept rhythm with his pulse
He wasn't sure anymore
Of what was true or false
He'd been dreaming about Elvis
Or someone or something
He was tired of his life
But he wasn't tired of jumping.

Displaced
When did we lose our way?
Displaced
We want to stay in everyday
We used to cry out loud together

Now we cry quietly alone
Displaced
We've no place........ like home.

Later in the dead of night a paranoid parent's pondering plight….

Woke up got out of bed
With visions of you rioting in my head
Where will you live and what will you do?
Are you safe or have the demons taken over you?
Where's your comforting emoji or thumbs up
Just something to soothe my fears and hang ups
I panicked and called you when I should have been asleep
And your voicemail answered before I could speak
"I'm not here right now just leave a message after the bleeps"

(97) Now You See Me, Now You Don't - 2021 (page 186)

I was in the tower block that burned
It happened when your back was turned
I'm the child that was a mistake
From a broken home and needing a break
I'm in the subway singing the blues
Later in the station I'll be shining your shoes
I'm the lonely widow at her husband's wake
I'm the missing person at the bottom of a lake
And I'm the refugee squeezed onto the boat
Now you see me now you don't.

I'm the late night crawler in the shadows of the street
I'm the girl on minimum wage offering you a seat
I'm working very hard to make trainers for your feet
Sometimes you hear I'm not well or had enough to eat
I'm the displaced mother, child or father

Following another civil war or natural disaster
I'm another statistic on a chart
Who can't afford the operation for their heart
I'm the so called traitor hanging from a rope
Now you see me now you don't.

I'm the boy in the corner who's always on his own
I'm the girl at the party who always leaves alone
I'm the man in the grave nobody ever visits
I'm the woman at the bar getting lost in spirits
I'm the inmate feeling not quite right in the head
Who's slept a lifetime in the same room and bed
I live in social housing at the rough end of your town
I'm the nuclear shadow burnt into the ground
I'm the person at work that just can't cope
Now you see me now you don't.

I'm the face of this year's charity campaign
Next Christmas you just might see me again
I'm the sick child on comic relief
Whose parents live in a ghetto persecuted for their beliefs
I'm the girl left freezing in a trailer
From the other half of the world from across the equator
I'm the soldier left alone to stand
In the crossfire of Afghanistan
You say you care but when the time comes you won't
Now you see me now you don't.

(98) Look At Me - 2021 (page 187)

Behind every face there's some kind of pain
But that's not an open invitation to share it
Our personal woe is over exposed
Why do we feel the need to declare it?

Shiny and bright, naked and bare
We wear our hearts on our sleeves
But unnecessary, like a fashion accessory
What are we really hoping to achieve?

We stand to attention, yearn attention and share a tension
That's really too personal and private to publicly mention
Then these online confessions get a chorus of approval
From the connected platforms of the ensemble communal
But this choir isn't really singing songs of praise
It's just another symptom of our sad malaise.

Look at me and like me, we say
And leave a positive remark
We need a regular affirmation
We need house points, grades and marks
Look at me - and my inclusion and diversity
Look at me - and my general modernity
Look at me - I've been to university
Look at me - I'm in touch with my sexuality
Look at me - and my highbrow morality
Look at me - and my liberal normality
Look at me - and my neurodiversity
Look at me - and my profound lack of energy
Look at me - and my quirky idiosyncrasies
Look at me - and my needy personality
Look at me - I'm both woke and angry
Look at me - please click me and swipe me
Look at me - please tick me and like me
Look at me and my problems with mental health
Look at me because I can't stand to look at myself.

Epilogue

As you get older you spend more time trying to find yourself
Because you keep forgetting where you've put it......

So I'm organising a search party
With my friends from Pilates
I've got peanuts coated in wasabi
And a bottle of nice Chianti
We'll gather round to hear my story
All my problems and painful glory
This my drama and I don't care if it's a sin
To be the only character I'm emotionally invested in.

(99) My Last Big Failure Or Last Big Mistake -2022 (page 189)

Will this be...
My last big failure or last big mistake?
The last precious thing I'm ever going to break?
My last bad deal in which I have a bad stake?
The last sick joke that I narrate?
My last stupid thought for heaven's sake?
The last boss that I unfairly berate?
My last time to slam on the brakes?
The last useless thing I have to undertake?
The last time I make up something fake?
My last family schism and emotional quake?
The last occasion of unwelcome heartache?
My last big problem and bad headache?
The last prescription or placebo I take?
My last conversation with a rattlesnake?
The last sordid thing in which I partake?
My last unnecessary coffee break?
Or my last big failure or last big mistake?

Or perhaps there's a few more to go?

(100) Run - 2022 (page 190)

I learnt to run when I was just two
Always running to catch up with you
I was running before I could count or chew
Running was all I ever wanted to do.

When I was older I put on my running shoes
Sometimes I just felt I could run for miles
Running to every lesson in every classroom
Running up and down every shopping aisle.

At twenty one, I ran into you
And that's when I ran into my fate
You were smart and you ran rings around me
We'd both run for office and you'd be my running mate.

Together we hit the ground running
We were going to take the money and run
But instead we ran up debts we couldn't pay
The cash ran out and soon we were washed up and done.

We ran our business into the ground
We were running up against the receivers
You were starting to feel run down
I was running a debilitating fever.

The course of true love never does run smooth
And soon ours just ran out of steam
We couldn't hold with the hares and run with hounds
Unlike Tom Petty, we weren't runnin' down a dream.

I heard you'd been planning to run away
Leaving, one evening, via the airport runway
That's why they call you runaround Sue
I should have always known you'd be a little runaway.

I wanted to run for cover
Running scared, as I watched my fortunes plummet
I'd been running in circles and I'd run out of gas
But I knew life's a gauntlet and I still had to run it.

They say still waters run deep
But mine were running with anxiety
I'll just have to learn to run with it
As it had always run in the family
(Like noses).

(101) It's Only Ourselves - 2022 (page 191)

It's only ourselves that feel this pain
It's only ourselves that hurt again
It's only ourselves that can win or lose
It's only ourselves that can sing the blues
It's only ourselves that feel ashamed
It's only ourselves to blame.

It's only ourselves that can negotiate peace
It's only ourselves that clear the streets
It's only ourselves that declare a war
It's only ourselves that have done this before
It's only ourselves that can fan the flames
It's only ourselves to blame.

It's only ourselves on our own terms
It's only ourselves that crash and burn

It's only ourselves that keep on grieving
It's only ourselves that don't stop believing
It's only ourselves that suffer or reign
It's only ourselves to blame.

It's only ourselves that stay up at night
It's only ourselves that shake with fright
It's only ourselves that get filled with hate
It's only ourselves that destroy what we create
It's only ourselves that kill and maim
It's only ourselves to blame.

(102) The Cold Raw Wind And Rain- 2022 (page 192)

I think it might rain today
The sky is looking overcast and grey
The clouds are rolling in and the portents look grim
I can feel an icy wind and rain about to set in
I'm staying put and will continue hiding
I won't be throwing caution to the wind
But nothing will be gained, if it's here I remain
And don't face the cold raw wind and rain.

I don't like heavy weather showers
Or when the rain goes on for hours
Is it a sign of impending misfortune?
Warning me to exercise caution
And keep things in proportion
Or is this just pathetic fallacy?
I know misery loves company
But my life can't be spent gazing from behind the double glazing
I must open up the pane to the cold raw wind and rain.

I'm full of fears and my hands are clenched

I avoid the thought of getting drenched
But that means a life that can only fizzle
Because I'm afraid of the heavy drizzle
Or becoming cold and shrivelled
I know some of us just shelter and cower
We want to avoid ever getting caught in a cold shower
But to live the answer's plain, you've got to do it and then do it again
Embrace the cold raw wind and rain.

And also extreme heat too.

Art And Illumination

(103) The Bernese Oberland - 2006 (page 195)

Bernese Oberland
You frighten me
With your ice palaces
And insane gradients
From the calm translucence of the Thun
To the dizzying height of the Sphinx in the winter sun.

I was drinking coffee in an Interlaken café
I was sailing across the green hue of lake Brienzee
I saw climbers defying Eiger's rock
I was catching my breath, eleven thousand feet above sea level
On the Jungfraujoch.

(104) The Louvre - 2007 (page 195)

Artemis and Hermes observing a battle between Macedonian warriors
The disconcerting smile of La Gioconda
The golden apartments of Napoleon the 3rd
The lacquered finishes and objet d'art
Leonardo's Virgin and Child
The Venus de Milo looking on from afar
Liberté rising from the brush of Delacroix
The writings and drawings from Mesopotamia
The rock art of Mauritania
Jean Baptiste's drafts and sculptures
All manner of artefacts from ancient cultures
Gold leaf on the ceilings and depictions of the scriptures
Gabrielle d'Estrées and one of her sisters
Mummified remains in honour of Osiris
Tableaux depicting the arrival of Isis
Tapestry narrations of biblical Apocalypse
Brush strokes ignite the flight of the Phoenix

Precious, enlightened and so often visited
This treasure trove beneath the glass panes of the Pyramid.

(105) Eyes - 2007 (page 196)

Red eyes
Green eyes
Ideal eyes
Material eyes
Sad eyes
Real eyes
Scandal eyes
Stable eyes
And great big round eyes
That glow
Surrounded by eyeshadow
Tearful eyes
Terrif eyes
Advert eyes
Pulver eyes
Ion eyes
Vandal eyes
Monetar eyes
Canon eyes
Woman eyes
Local eyes
Chast eyes
National eyes
Personal eyes
System eyes
Snake eyes
Popular eyes
Moisture eyes
Black eyes

Revital eyes
Legal eyes
Mesmer eyes
Weapon eyes
Cats eyes
Cannibal eyes
Neutral eyes
Modern eyes
Capital eyes
Visual eyes
Enfranch eyes
Blue eyes
Familiar eyes
Bastard eyes
Computer eyes
Immortal eyes
Penal eyes
And Vapour eyes
Eyes down - the eyes have it.

Eye search
Therefore eyebrows.

(106) Goodbye Maria - 2003 (page 197)

Goodbye Maria
Your sad and stirring refrain
Still fills me with wonder and delight
But I think it's time for me to leave tonight.

Goodbye Maria
I was just a young boy
In the Odeon Leicester square
Torn by the three verses and middle eight of Somewhere.

Goodbye Maria
Your lilting harmonies
Your major and minor keys
But a Puerto Rican girl like you will leave me lonely.

Goodbye Maria
I made a vow
To take you somewhere, someday, somehow
Before the curtain closes and we take a bow
Is it only death that can part us now?

Goodbye Maria
You saw the better part of me
When I was young and had an innocent dreaming piety
You tell me something is coming, something good
I still want to believe it and I wish I could.

Goodbye Maria
For just a brief moment the world was full of light
So if I dream, I'll dream of you tonight
We'll be wild, we'll be bright
With time for each other and time to care
Time to learn and time to spare.....
But I lost my way and you are still hiding somewhere.

Goodbye Maria
You were then at your most beautiful
And I was at my most sincere
Even now your music still moves me to tears
Perhaps it's the most beautiful sound in the world I'll ever hear.

(107) Roma - 2019 (page 199)

Lasagne and linguini
Pizzas and homemade spaghetti
Murano glass and souvenirs
Cobbled streets from bygone years
And there's the Trevi fountain
Another coin gets thrown in
A young child holding a lemon gelato
Wooden carvings of Pinocchio and Geppetto
Rich man, poor man, beggar man and thief
Their stories framed in stone and gold leaf
Their secrets stored in the dark caverns of churches and museums
Or in the ruins of the Colosseum
Pagan ancestry and Hebrew mythology
With just a dash of Greek philosophy
In the Botticelli frescoes
And the brush of Michelangelo
The ghosts of St Paul and St Peter
Haunt every chapel and Basilica
Outside dangerous drivers in fast cars
And girls that look like continental movie stars
Couples climb the Spanish steps
There are new loves, old loves and regrets
Climb up to where the Jasmine grows
Where you might be sold a lover's rose
Every street a story with something going on
Could be in a bar or restaurant
Or could be in the Pantheon
Roman Gods rubbing shoulders
With fashion brands and luggage holders
Roman slaves and Gladiators
Hanging out in the squares and piazzas
Or posing by the Tiber from a balcony

Thinking they might be Caesar or Mark Anthony

(108) It's All There - 2020 (page 200)

All the mysteries and controversies
The scapegoats and the tales
All the myths and the realities
All the loose ends and the trails
All the clues in the Da Vincis
The assassins and the kings
For every Oswald or Ruby
There's always someone conspiring
You want the facts laid bare?
Well..it's all there.

The meaning of the universe
The search for hell or heaven
Sinking the Titanic
What caused Nine Eleven
Digging up the Pharaohs
Murdering the Tsars
Landing on the moon
Trying to reach the stars
What, how, why and where?
Well..it's all there.

Nixon and Watergate
Archduke Ferdinand
Hitler's secret bunker
The abominable snowman
Studying Mark Chapman
And Martin Luther King
They thought they found Elvis
And the theory of everything

You need answers, you declare?
Well..it's all there.

Who killed Cock Robin?
Who shot JR ?
Who killed Butch and the Sundance kid?
Who drove the getaway car?
Who fired the rifle?
Who had the power?
Who murdered the princes
In the bloody tower?
Are there names you want to share?
Well...they're all there.

All the theories and philosophies
The fairy tales and spies
All the heroes and mediocrities
All the nursery rhymes and lies
All the buried treasures
The search for holy grails
All the UFO sightings
And leaked emails
You'll tell the truth you swear?
Well..it's all there.

(109) Tea - 2020 (page 201)

Black tea
White tea
Lemon tea
Special tea
Royal tea
Cruel tea
Gravi tea

Green tea
Eterni tea
Admiral tea
Uni tea
Para tea
Boston tea
Part tea
Nettle tea
Chari tea
Pu-erh tea
Puri tea
Rose tea
Senna tea
Sani tea
Facul tea
Complexi tea
Equala tea
Liber tea
Fraterni tea
Digni tea
Herbal tea
Chai tea
Trini tea
And all the way to Infini tea
Fancy a cup?

Sorry I know this poem isn't everyone's cup of tea.

(110) Buried Bodies - 2020 (page 202)

Some bodies
No bodies
Any bodies
Busy bodies

Anti bodies
Auntie bodies
Every bodies
Disem bodies
Beach bodies
Dog bodies
Em bodies
Fit bodies
Thin bodies
Super bodies
Buried bodies
...dig 'em up.

....a body of work.

(111) A Bolt Of Illumination - 2020 (page 203)

Let the faithful come and the citizens of expression
Take up your carving tools, your oils, your palettes and brushes
I need a bolt of illumination in this dark age twilight
I need the stab of exultation raised up by choirs of angels
I believe there's an eternal splendour
In the rock, the stone, the bronze and canvas
In abstract expressionism and post modernism
In the impressionists and the hedonists
In myths and legends and the earth and heavens
Give me sunflowers and stars
Give me drums and guitars
Let the great ideas come to me
Like apples falling from a tree
Build me temples to hope in the highest
Fill them with minds free and unbiased
Don't let them stop us
Creating our Magnum Opus

Let those iridescent rock pools of persistence
Become our call to arms, our piece de resistance
Let us bravely sing our cri de cœur
At each stage of our crusade and world tour
I want to hear the chanting of the believers and the pious
Venite adoremus *
And long may the energy of creation reign over us.

*Venite adoremus (come let us adore him)

(112) Double Red, White And Blue (The Love You Leave Behind) - 2022 (page 204)

<u>Side 1</u>

In my darkest hour
When I'm so tired
There are places I remember
Of magic and mystery
Like riding nowhere and not arriving
On a long and winding road
In a land of nowhere
Under a sky of diamonds.

There's an an ocean child
With seashell eyes and a windy smile
Holding flowers of yellow and green
In a yellow submarine
Floating across a green sea
Waves lapping against the cast iron shore
Near a field of strawberries.

I'm down on the ground
Under my favourite tree

In a wood from Norway
Misunderstanding all I see
Here comes the sun
Shining in a sky of blue
I know tomorrow may rain
So for now I'm following you
This is where the blackbirds sing
And there's beauty in every little thing.

Or let me take you down
To where I was born
In a lane, suburban and blue
Where there's a girl who tastes of honey
And carries a bag of chocolate cake
And says she still loves you
She's the girl with the sun in her eyes
She's a woman with a ticket to ride
Way down south to the snow peaked mountains
Where the world is spinning round
This is the colour of my dreams
In images of broken light
It doesn't matter if I'm wrong or right
They don't let me down
They get my feet back on the ground.

Side 2

These are the waves of joy
And pools of sorrow
Across my universe
Things are getting better
But they've been a whole lot worse.
I can see the sun coming

Above a host of swaying daisies
Singing their lazy song
I'm holding hands with a short haired girl
Who sometimes wears it twice as long
One day I'll be back again
I'm hoping it won't be long.

The wind is high and it blows my mind
It's been a long long time
So many tears I've been wasting
But not a second time.
It seems like years
Since it's been clear
That all I've got to do
Is think of love as something new
After all, it's only love and that is all
I know that it's a fool
Who plays it cool
By making his world a little colder
Or carries it on his shoulders.

So why on earth should I moan?
About the many times I've been alone
A blue mist around my soul
I even hated my rock and roll
But now I'm fixing that hole
And I know where I will go
Because when I'm home
Everything seems to be right
Life is very short
And there's no time to fuss and fight.

Side 3

All these years we've been wandering
With our children at our feet
Wondering why nobody told us
Half the world is only sleeping
While the other gently weeps
So let's all get up
We know what it feels like to be dead
Why be a fool or a rich man
When you can free your mind instead.

If you think you've lost your love
It's because you hid it away
If you think you're going to be sad
Then believe in yesterday
We should have known better
Afterall, tomorrow never comes
And there's nothing we can do
That can't be done
And there's no song we can sing
That can't be sung.

But you can't just buy love
You know what I mean
And if you're just giving money
You won't see me
Because it might be for people
With minds that hate
You've got to be a joker
If you've not learnt from that mistake
So let me tell you how it should be
And all the broken hearted people in the world agree
If we hold a hand and lend an ear
And don't sing out of key

Then at the count of four we can come together
And take a sad song and make it sound a whole lot better.

We can save the world with our love
It's in the things we've said today
And anytime we feel the pain
Let's promise we'll get back again
For us to lead a better life
We need to spread the word and think for ourselves
Is anyone going to listen to our story?
Because it's something we want to tell
Why write a sermon no one will hear
Or no one comes near
So before we get older
Losing our hair
Let's spread the word we're thinking of
Here, there and everywhere
Even if there's no reply
There's no good reason
For taking the easy way out
And if you ask me why
It's because this isn't the time to twist
It's the time to shout.

Side 4

Let's carry that weight on our shoulders
I'll pass it from me to you
I appreciate you being 'round to help
And if you help me I'll help you too
The long cold lonely winter is over
The endless rain has stopped
Our words have finally filled that paper cup.
It's time to pull our socks up

And help each other understand
Love is more than just holding hands
We can celebrate anything we want
And our kindness will linger on
We're getting back to where we belong.

Anytime you feel afraid
Or don't feel fine
Just call me, anytime
You know my name and number
I'm not the hurting kind
I can show you a better time
There's a place where we can go
Where living is easy with eyes closed
It's here the singers sing a song
And all the lonely people sing along
There are no angry young men of cruelty
Everyone can rattle their jewellery.
Sometimes it's all too much
I know what it is to be sad
But you can talk to me
And you know that can't be bad
Or if you want a revolution
It doesn't bother me
Because
The one thing I can tell you is...
We've got to be free.

I've got a feeling this time it's right
We're learning to fly
And the stars are shining bright
So unpack your case and disconnect the phone
As love has a nasty habit

Of disappearing overnight
It's a limitless undying love
That shines like a million suns
There's no I or Me or Mine
On a good day for sunshine
Because in the end
The love you seek and the love you find
Is equal to the love you leave behind.

(The Beatles - the soundtrack to my life- thank you)

(113) Heart Of My Universe -2022 (page 210)

You're the shiver in the back of my spine
The aching in my heart I don't mind
You've been there nearly all of my time
When I lift up your veil I'm drawn to your flame
You're in every precious tear I should shed
Your last refrain still plays in my head
You shine but I'm not easily led
You've left a smouldering pain and you're burning again.

You should be in every way
The best bit of my day
In all the space I traverse
You're still the heart of my universe.

You're the melody to my sun going down
You're my elegy when no one's around
You're a violin symphony that's playing for me in A minor key
You're so near but so out of reach
You don't need the power of speech
Everything you play is in tune and in harmony, way beyond me.

You should be in every way
The best bit of my day
In all the space I traverse
You're still the heart of my universe.

You're the aria wrenching my soul
My yesterdays have taken their toll
If I could go back to the start I wouldn't do things the same
The power of your expression is pure
I know your truth will endure
Your songs of sadness reign, so play them again, stripped back and plain.

You should be in every way
The best bit of my day
In all the space I traverse
You're still the heart of my universe.

You're a shiver in search of a spine
I really hope that it's mine
My circadian rhythms play in my dreams but not in my days
You're kind warm, bright and bold
I should be too but I'm cold
I'm the owner of rolls royce heart that just won't spark
And the chauffeur's away, why didn't he stay?

You should be in every way
The best bit of my day
In all the space I traverse
You're still the heart of my universe.

Not Feeling Ok

(114) The Chicken Pox Blues -1994 (page 213)

There was one on my neck
Small round and red
It didn't mean a thing
Till I felt one on my head
I was starting to sweat
And starting to chill
My skin was tingling
I was feeling pretty ill
I've had my share of cough and colds and nasty little flus
But no one ever told me about the chicken pox blues.

...and what was only one spot
Became a family
They were breeding like chickens
In a chicken factory
They were climbing up my leg
Running down my arm
There was nowhere on my body
That didn't have one
They come in different sizes
Different shapes and different hues
No one ever told me about the chicken pox blues.

I had pains in my head
Sickness in my gut
I was looking like a Pizza
That you get in Pizza Hut
My face was erupting
I was a viral stew
My nerves were revolting
In a symptom led coup
I couldn't eat solids or smell or taste or chew

No one ever told me about the chickenpox blues.

These spots are amazing
They have personality
Some are red and tender
Some grow in twos and threes
Some are brown and crusty
Some start, then fall to bits
Some don't even start at all
And some are painful little shits
I should have had this earlier and not at thirty two
No one ever told me about the chicken pox blues.

(115) Who's Driving The Car? - 1995 (page 214)

I've been drinking beyond my fill
There are beer stains on the window-sill
I ate till I made myself ill
Drank till I could no longer feel
Life no longer seems to hold a thrill
Every venture seems uphill
I've been out with every Jack and Jill
I've got my foot on the pedal but my hand's not on the wheel.

A walk to the shops is an act of will
None of my friends ever seem real
The days roll on but everything's still
The places that I go to are run of the mill
I'm never inspired, I have no zest or zeal
I'm on an up escalator heading downhill
I should make a pact with the Devil
But I'm too tired to do a deal
I've got my foot on the pedal but my hand's not on the wheel.

Too many TV dinners and pills
Too many memories of the same ordeal
I have too much time to waste or kill
You'll always find me with my snout in the swill
What a piece of art I am - surreal
Better go find another drink to spill
And one more heart to break or steal
I've got my foot on the pedal but my hand's not on the wheel.

(116) Unfortunate Circumstances - 2015 (page 215)

So here we are again dear friend and neighbour
Meeting again in calamity
Your hopeless bone framed stare
Tells me we won't get out of this easily
Unbelievably
We'd assumed if we prayed frequently
And lived our lives decently
We'd get our reward and earn our stars
But that's not how it's played out so far
There's nothing that's a certainty
It's an absurdity
We resist this conclusion so determinedly.

There's a black tide building up behind a heart shaped dam
We want to scream and get as far away from this as we can
We pray for relief in our unfolding fate
But there are no guarantees it won't be one we hate,

So will we stay and take a chance?
Take our troubles to the next cosmic tea dance
Take our steps and exchange furtive glances
With the suitors of our unfortunate circumstances.

There are no free rides or sacred cows
We can only control the seconds we have now
All we really have and all that's really true
Is in this moment what we say and do.

(117) Sickness (in two parts) - 2015 (page 216)

Sickness part 1 - 1823

I was fine ambling from meal to meal
Lost in the detail of my day
Feeling fine and well
Happy that the river flowed my way
Annoyed when it didn't
Free as a bird
Flitting from word to word
Trying to impress
Until I met Sickness.

He was just a niggling presence
I no longer felt my best
I felt chills and an aching
Caused by this unwelcome guest
But with glass half full
I was solid and resisting
Until my head welled up
And my eyes began misting
I knew who he was and how he wanted to be addressed
And he was called Sickness.

"Please allow me to introduce myself"
Said my cruel unwelcome friend
"Let me take you by the hand
And together lets descend

I've known so many people
Across your biological history
And after all this time together
You don't know how to treat me
No need to look your Sunday best
For Sickness".

And so we took our steps
Into the first circle of despair
I said goodbye to kith and kin
And all the world out there
So armed with panaceas
Remedies and good luck charms
Placebos, pills and potions
Witchcraft, drugs and balms
I was ready now to take the tests
Of Sickness.

For five days and nights
We wrestled in feverish embrace
I poured so much into that fight
I was nearly laid to waste
My circadian rhythms
Were out of control
There was darkness in my head
A deep, dank hole
And always as God is my witness
I saw the unrelenting smile of Sickness.

No one have I known so closely
Or shared so much of me
We'd become so well acquainted
In our morbid intimacy

It has been said that it gets dark
Before the dawn begins to rise
For twas then the morning light
Woke my crusted aching eyes
You'd taken your leave but left unfinished business
And I'm still haunted by the memory of Sickness.

Now I'm on the lookout for your symptoms to manifest
So I'm ready once again to battle with Sickness.

Sickness part 2 - 2023

The scans and the prognosis
The self talk and hypnosis
The long haul thrombosis
The worries and neuroses
This sick and painful industry
Which is my medicinal history
A troubled untidy litany
Of surgery and sympathy
And other pyrrhic victories
That are fatally contradictory
And lead me to confess
I'm still a physical mess
And even though I protest
He still prays on my weakness
And never let's me rest
He won't be second best
And in this mortal contest
The winner you can guess....
With worryingly success
Will in the end be Sickness.

(118) Not Like You - 2018 (page 219)

Your morning starts with a coffee in your favourite cup
You might do something new today but you can't make your mind up
Your friends are heading south and your boy is heading off too
You'd think that he'd be over this but then he's not like you.

Your sister tries to talk to you while you're making other plans
You spend all day alone thinking no one understands
Your days float by, in shades of black and then in shades of blue
This all feels so wrong to me but then I'm not like you.

You used to be the brightest moon around the orbit of the sun
Poised before the pistol signalled you to run
Did you cover too much ground, bit off more than you could chew?
You're too content sitting on the bench and I know that's not like you.

You think that being a member of the senior officers' club
Means that it's acceptable to simply just give up
Will you let me tell you something; can I share my point of view?
I can see you're really hiding and I know that's not like you.

You're drifting from the busy shore in your makeshift craft
When I said that you might sink, well you just sat and laughed
You say you're fine and riding high but you know that's not true
You're turning into someone but someone not like you.

(119) Self Harm -2018 (page 219)

He cut the word oblivion on his arm
She drank too much to keep herself calm
He couldn't say the things that were on his mind
He's given up trying to be kind
She gave up on him, then she gave up on food

It was a lot more than just being in a bad mood
All alone in her room she stayed
Trying to hide her feelings and her rib cage
Nasty gin hidden in a flask
Trying to wear a sobriety mask
Liquid fire, dampening pain
Secret moments to start drinking again
Commercial collapse, cuts and confusion
Public opinion so hurtful and bruising
Up at night she just can't sleep
She craves temazepam not numbers of sheep
Nicotine on his fingers, coffee on his breath
Two shakes away from living, one shake from death
All the hours God sent him lost in a flash
All leading towards his next car crash
Laid out, tongue tied, in need of a nurse
She's going to put her whole life into reverse
Morbid curiosity from their friends and neighbours
Keen to see how far they've fallen from favour
Looking for the lines, looking for the scars
Tales from the bedroom and gossip in the bars
About their force fed fluctuating wire frames
And their pathological predilection for pincers and pain
Self absorbed, solo, siloed and stuck
Lost labelled and out of luck.

(120) I Can't Stand The Sight Of Blood - 2020 (page 220)

I want to be in a world without blood
It makes me sick that my veins are full of the stuff
It's thick and red like trench war mud
I can't stand the sight of blood.

There's blood in my eyes and blood in my ears

There's blood in all the things that I fear
It's in the hearts of the loathed and of the loved
I can't stand the sight of blood.

It's a most disagreeable thing to me
It's a sign of my pending mortality
It can start as a trickle then turn to a flood
I can't stand the sight of blood.

There's always someone making a sacrifice
Giving blood comes at the highest price
And we can't ever seem to give enough
I can't stand the sight of blood.

It's there in all the contracts we sign
It's in the work we do and the ties that bind
It's in the rhythm of every loving kiss or hug
I can't stand the sight of blood.

It's in all the bodies that have been cut and diced
It's in the cup that captured the sacrament of Christ
It's in everyone, both virtuous and corrupt
I can't stand the sight of blood.

Each day someone has to bleed and spill their guts
For another evil genius they distrust
Who is driven by a wanton bloodlust
I can't stand the sight of blood.

(I can't stand heights either).

(121) I Feel Like A Number - 2020 (page 221)

I feel like a number

I might be a three or a two
My days are numbered
But yours are too.

You know my serial number
And it's not a cushy number
So show me the numbers
Because I've got your number.

I was drinking seven up
From the seven eleven
I was watching Formula one
I was three steps from heaven.

I was public enemy number one
Now I'm number nine
So play me another number
Because I'm putting my numbers on the line

I'm all sixes and sevens
And in two minds
One over the eight
But dressed up to the nines.

I'm killing two birds with one stone
Getting back to square one
Meeting my opposite number
Who's unlucky for some.

I want to kick the numbers
Those numbers not in my favour
There is always strength in numbers
Until your number is up.

I'm going to count my blessings
So I'm counting on you
It's the thought that counts
And all the thinking and counting we do.

(122) Dead - 2020 (page 223)

In the Dead of night
The night of the living Dead
He got there Dead on arrival
Dead easy
He'd been in a Dead end for too long
Flogging a Dead horse
But he was Dead calm now
Taking Dead centre aim
To take them down - stone Dead
Dead to rights
It was a Dead cert
And he was Dead set.

He was Dead ringer
For Deadpool
He'd written himself a Dead letter
About his Dead end jobs
Being a roadie for the Grateful Dead
And selling Dead parrots
Across the Dead sea
But it was all Dead in the water
His life was as Dead as a dodo
Too long holding onto the Dead man's handle
Too long living on Dead end street
Too long buying things Dead cheap
He wasn't going to play Dead anymore

This wouldn't end in a Dead heat
And he wouldn't be seen Dead here
This time he would drop Dead
Or be a Deadhead
He wanted this over - Dead and buried
Either Dead or alive
And if they tried to take him down
It would be over his Dead body.

(123) Emergency Room - 2020 (page 224)

I'm feeling tachy and I'm over one sixty
My BPM's has had an erratic history
I need a CBC and a chem seven
My pupils are blown and I'm three shots from heaven.

This world is wed to the captains of industry
But I'm not in love and they don't mean that much to me.

No money and no urgency
No one getting an apology
Nobody getting fixed for free
We're all heading down to the emergency room.

He's got a gunshot wound to the head and chest
He's lying on a stretcher waiting for some tests
He needs an ABG and his BP is falling
They need to intubate soon but the system is stalling.

He'd had a fall out with his estranged lover
If he'd had his time again he'd have paid for cover.

No shame and no sympathy
Unless you've private equity

To pay for treatment with some dignity
We're all heading down to the emergency room.

She's DNR because it's cheaper that way
If she could be DOA there'd be nothing to pay
She's an MVA with hypertension
She's got acute MI and a widow's pension

Her kids feel she's become a bit of a burden
She knows this condition will only worsen.

No one making this a priority
Apart from a consultancy
Specialising in redundancy
We're all heading down to the emergency room.

A second rate state led by welfare traders
We're all up the creek without a respirator
Past broken promises continue to linger
The political equivalent of the middle finger.

Making policy on the hoof
Being economical with the truth.

No time now to put it right
No one taking up the fight
The red cross pales against the white
We're all heading down to the emergency room.

(BPM = beats per minute / CBC = complete blood count / Chem 7 = medical blood tests / ABG =
arterial blood gases / BP = blood pressure / DNR = do not resuscitate / DOA = dead on arrival
/ MVA = motor vehicle accident / Acute MI = Acute myocardial infarction)

(124) Para -2021 (page 226)

I'm feeling paralysed
Trapped within my own parameters
I'm stalked by parasites
And I'm victim to paranormal activity
My life is a paradox
Wrapped up in a paradigm
There's no escape
I've got no parachute
I just want to hide
Under my parasol.

I think there might be a paratrooper
Patrolling parallel to my house
Perhaps I'm just being paranoid
I need paracetamols
To calm my paramania
And predilection for paraffin
And pouring it on my paraphernalia
Wow ....I'm on the edge of a parapet.

I wish I just could just paraglide through life
To paraphrase a paragraph from a parable
One thing's for certain this is no paradise.

(125) Bad Time - 2021 (page 226)

I'd had a bad day
At Black Rock
Life was a bad dream
I was from bad stock
Born under a bad sign
And a bad curse

Things had gone from bad to worse
I'd come from a bad home
I was bad to the bone
The bearer of bad news
In a bad position
Getting bad reviews
I was in bad condition
I looked like a bad apple
Nursing a bad head
I was a bad joke
And smelt like a bad egg
I had a bad dog
With bad breath
He left a bad taste in my mouth
And had run up bad debts.

I'd made a bad turn
I was in a bad way
It was a bad winter
And I was having a bad hair day
Things were so bad
My bad temper getting the better of me
It was my bad
I'd chosen to be in bad company
I had bad friends
With bad ideas
We were stuck in bad jobs
And bad careers
I'd made a bad move
I was in a bad spot
Still I was making the best of a bad lot.

On reflection

How bad is bad ?
Is it when things are bad but not terrible?
Or when they're not great but bearable?
Is a bad day not too bad or not bad at all?
Comme ci, comme ça; not awful but just not exceptional
Or is it when you're feeling pretty bad or not too good
Or feeling a whole lot worse than you thought you should?

(126) I Just Can't Let It Be -2022 (page 228)

I just can't let it be
Like in the song written by Lennon and McCartney
When I find myself in times of trouble
I just simmer with anxiety
In my many hours of darkness
When I mull over my actions and plans
Mother Mary doesn't come to me
Instead I reach for Diazepam
I hear no words of wisdom
There is no light that shines on me
Friends say I shouldn't worry
But I just can't let it be
I hope one day I will see
That all the worst things are behind me
But dark thoughts keep haunting me
I'm lost in my low spectrum OCD
And I just can't let it be

(127) Bad Dreams - 2023 -(page 228)

As I dream the night away
That's when the bad things come out to play
Phantoms of my past and future
Half baked ghosts of memory and rumour

Whispers and strands of the phantasmagorical
With or without meaning or perhaps allegorical
Engendering emotions that rarely surface
Why are they here and what need do they service?
These demons of my latent imagination
Perform their dance macabre in cruel rotations
In conspiratorial cycles of intimidation
They are masters of movement and manipulation
They strut, they step, they pirouette
Some moves I remember and some I forget
They are voices calling from far away
Like the distant pecking of birds of prey
They cast shadows and bring out the bones
Of a mad montage that I must endure alone
Once they start I can't interrupt
The only way out is for me to wake up
So while I sleep they set up their stall
From the Freudian labyrinth of my memory pool
Collecting my real or imagined fears and follies
In their surrealistic shopping trolleys
There are.....

      Zombie wraiths that float and bend
      Staircase falls that never end
      Rotting bodies in garden sheds
      Mother's secret, Father's dread
      The Queen, King and Jack of Hearts
      Catching me eating all the tarts
      Then I'm hung before the verdict
      I guess it's because I deserved it
      Being somewhere I don't belong
      Arriving at school with no trousers on
      I'm the source of work's derision
      Sitting an exam without revision

A dwarf hands me something soft
It's green and wet and I can't rub it off
Weals that peel cover my back
Trapped in a cage filled with rats
Rooms with doors that never open
Grinning skulls that are cracked and broken
Toothless bullies make me cry
I try to run but my legs are tied
A priest possessed and adversarial
Presiding over my premature burial
Driving in the deepest night
With no cats eyes or head lights
Goblins bare their sharpened teeth
Drooling over raw red meat
The count descends the darkened stairs
Licks his lips and smooths his hair
Sharpening the surgeon's knives
Someone screaming 'it's alive'
I do my best to shield my eyes
But I cannot move I'm paralyzed
My heart is beating like a cattle drum
Something wicked this way comes
Headlong into terror I descend
Only by waking will this nightmare end.
Then suddenly I'm awake
Shocked back to existence
My mind took all it could take
And this nightmare lost its resistance
But why do I still feel troubled?
Why do I still feel strife?
I pray these night time apparitions
Aren't the shadows and visions of my real life.

Religion And Philosophy

(128) There's A God -1985 (page 232)

There's a God for everybody
There's a God for everyone
Whether you are wise or righteous
Or whether you're old or young
There's God who loves the healthy
There's a God who loves the sick
There's a God who needs magicians
To prepare for his next trick
There's a God who wants his vengeance
And one thing that's for sure
There's a God.

There's a God who gives us dinner
There's a God who pours us tea
There's a God who pays our wages
There's a God for you and me
There's a God who lights the candle
There's a God who starts the war
There's a God who steals your wallet
Leaves you bleeding on the floor
There's a God who shares misfortune
And one thing that's for sure
There's a God.

There's a God in every fire
There's a God in every plague
There's a God in every fashion
There's a God in every rage
There's a God who loves the wealthy
There's a God who loves the poor
There's a God in every prison
He's broken every law

There's a God on every jury
And one thing that's for sure
There's a God.

There's a God in times of weakness
There's a God in times of need
There's a God for every leader
When their city's under siege
There's a God for America
There's a God for Japan
There's a God for Indonesia
There's a God for Afghanistan
There's a God for every refugee
And one thing that's for sure
There's a God.

There's a God who needs your contact
There's a God who needs your soul
There's a God whose only purpose
Is to fill your spiritual hole
There's a God who'll give you money
There's a God who'll give you guns
There's God who'll give you anything
Including his only son
There's a God because we need him
And one thing that's for sure
There's a God.

(129) The Saviour Of The World (or visions of Enobarbus) -2002 (page 233)

Istanbul 12.15, a Greek orthodox church
Burning blossom on the stairs, freeloaders at work
Static on the radio, black crows in the air

233

Queues at the embassy around the town square
Snow melting in the morning with the rising Orient sun
Glacier in the distance, wolves on the run
Lightning over cornfields to the west of Santa Fe
Storm clouds are gathering; the rain is here to stay.

Idle words along the highway, messages at dawn
A nurse is counting contractions to a new life being born
She sits upon a burnished throne, a worm around it curled
Everybody's waiting for the saviour of the world.

From a missile base in Cuba they're estimating the enemy's proximity
In a small town in Oslo they're re-enacting the nativity
There are Doctors and Philosophers redefining the world's narrative
A collection of conclusions that are merely comparative
A priest is heating instruments to numerically score
A bar code on the child born behind the stable door
In a cowshed by a temple under a blazing sun
Shepherds watch for salvation hoping there is one.

Idle words along the highway, messages at dawn
A nurse is counting contractions to a new life being born
She sits upon a burnished throne, a worm around it curled
Everybody's waiting for the saviour of the world.

Purple grapes upon the vine, skins about to burst
Black tails and hobnail boots follow a passing hearse
An aeroplane lands at Tel Aviv, passengers alight
Fireworks and gelatine explode in the feral night
You worship and despise the man that you have forsaken
You want to call him thief but you don't know what he's taken
You walk in his shadow but fear what he's awakened
You hope that he will save you but dread that you're mistaken.

Idle words along the highway, messages at dawn
A nurse is counting contractions to a new life being born
She sits upon a burnished throne, a worm around it curled
Everybody's waiting for the saviour of the world.

You keep one eye on your children and the other on your possessions
In the hope you can protect them from society's obsessions
While the lunatic fringe of the minority faction
Are hiding and waiting for a unilateral reaction
Matadors dance with red flags waving
Allied higher ground looks set to cave in
We plan to protect life but then we postpone it
Can't decide if we want to kill it, preserve it or clone it.

Idle words along the highway, messages at dawn
A nurse is counting contractions to a new life being born
She sits upon a burnished throne, a worm around it curled
Everybody's waiting for the saviour of the world.

The grey thin skin between real and opinion
A gossamer surface to hide personal oblivion
There is ne'er so empty in Antarctica or the Saharan wastes
As the search for truth or justice or defining God's face
She sailed a ship from Mozambique to the Iberian peninsular
Her words were sharp, her feelings raw, her position was irregular
She stood upon the crows nest, offered the elements her charms
Hoping to drown in the eyes of the world and die in its arms.

Idle words along the highway, messages at dawn
A nurse is counting contractions to a new life being born
She sits upon a burnished throne, a worm around it curled
Everybody's waiting for the saviour of the world.

John 4:42 *'They said to the woman, "It is no longer because of what you said that we believe, for we have heard for ourselves, and we know that this is indeed the Saviour of the world'.*

(130) Easter -2004 (page 236)

I came back from the dead
Now you celebrate me with an Easter Egg
They nailed my hands to the cross
The sentiment of that event has since been lost
I carried that cross upon my back
And now you worry about where the Easter eggs are stacked
I now look back in retrospect
And wonder was it worth all this celebration of chocolate?

(131) My 3 o'clock With Jesus -2005 (page 236)

I was sipping a chilled glass of Chardonnay
Inside the London Hard Rock café
He walked in and gave me a smile
I hadn't seen him in a while
He joined me and pulled up a chair
It must be hard being recognised everywhere
He placed on the table his crown of thorns
His clothes looked a little jaded and worn
But I guess when you've just been resurrected
You're going to look a little disconnected.
"You know it ain't easy" he said
"You know how hard it can be
The way things are going they're going to crucify me"
We both rolled up with laughter
And raised a glass to the hereafter.

Holy moly!

(132) Turn - 2006 (page 237)

I took a turn for the worse
Was it a wrong turn?
Or a funny turn?
I'm trying to turn a corner
But I can't seem to turn it around
I don't want turn it up
Or turn it down
Turn the tide
Turn the tables
Or turn a blind eye
It's a turn up for the books
This turn of events
It's now time for me to turn
Queen's evidence.

You say you turn if you want to
An interesting turn of phrase
I'd love to turn you on
So please don't turn away
The world keeps turning
Turning and turning in the widening gyre
As we turn the heat up higher
No one's turning the other cheek
Or turning over a new leaf
Our plans are turning sour
And the clocks keep turning back an hour
And at the turn of this century
We'll all turn eventually
And turn likely on each other
While you're turning into your Mother

...still one good turn deserves another.

(133) I'm Not Sure About Christmas -2006 (page 238)

I was notified today
That Christmas is on its way
Soon the boys of the NYPD choir
Will be singing "Galway Bay"
I'm hanging my stocking on the wall
But it's DPD not Santa that will call
I don't go out shopping anymore
Everything is delivered to my door
With all the packing, polystyrene and tape
I'm pleased I have a Christmas break.

I used to hope for snowflakes and Santa Claus
But now it's for a pudding with an orange stuffed to its core
Available only on eBay as the shops don't have them any more
Heston Blumenthal has a lot to answer for
They say Christmas is all around me
But to be honest only in "Love Actually"
And in the bit where Bill Nighhy
Tells Ant or Dec what they least expect
That they should become rock stars
And get their drugs for free
Christmas isn't just sweet and pretty
Or a fairytale in New York City
We won't swig Coke in a land faraway
Or hear the bells ring out on Christmas Day
For some it's a time they dread and hate
They pray to God for the great escape.

I nearly got run over by a boy on a bike
A young lout drunk on discount Tesco beer
Perhaps he thought he was walking on air
Bin bags full of turkey bones

Rubbish piled outside our homes
The perennial choral from Aled Jones
The carol singing hooligans at my front door
That's why I'm not sure about Christmas anymore.

(134) The Forbidden Zone -2007 (page 250)

Mock bodies crucified on makeshift crosses
Positioned on the edge of the precipice
To ward away the inquisitive and the curious
A dry heat permeated up from the ground
As cracks like veins spread from the source of the darkness
Best leave well alone
An old jeep carrier lay burnt out by the sun
Covered in sand
It looked as though it had grown from the rocks
An explosion flashed in a cloudless thunderous sky
Above the hidden caves dug in the Eilat mountains by Bedouin tribesman
Housing rotting scrolls foreshadowing a vision of Paimon
Who would rise from the ruins of an ancient alcázar
With a snake in one hand and a sickle in the other
A bitter war would rage
As the sun baked the earth
Angry in the sky and blazing.

(135) The Black Cross Freighter - or the Cook, the Boatswain and the Captain's Master - 2007 (page 239)

The Black Cross freighter left port in early June
It sailed through restless weathers under a quarter moon
It carried a cursed cargo and a troubled full man crew
An unholy fog was gathering as a storm began to brew.

The Captain was a godless man with no allegiance to a creed

There were signs of impending danger of which he took no heed
Consumed in his ambition and the search for fame or treasure
He'd take the path to hell or wherever took his pleasure.

He kept one eye on insurgents and another on his purse
Some crew wanted to take the ship, it's direction to reverse
The Boatswain of the vessel would lead this secret mutiny
And each day try to dodge the Captain's intense scrutiny.

The Cook prepared salted beef and numerous provisions
The crew sang a sea shanty with joyous derision
As the Captain passed through shadows with a cautious strut
And in the dark his 2nd officer's throat he untimely cut.

The Boatswain's broken body was hauled to the upper deck
Flying pests and scavengers fed from the wound in his neck
The Captain had hit hard and fast and established his position
He thought he'd quelled the rebels and silenced the opposition.

Several ghostly figures seemed to float across the stern
Or was it the oncoming mists as the climate took a turn
A single gnarled figure croaked from a ragged shawl
"We're in the 9th circle of hell, heaven help us all".

The Master, a God fearing man, discovered the bloody knife
He knew it was the Captain's and had taken the Boatswain's life
Oh sweet revenge was blooming in the Master's heart
The Captain's lead he would usurp and blow his brain apart.

Laid still the evil cargo but growing hateful and diseased
Accursed and despicable and on the crew's dark deeds it feeds
The Master scheming, snarling, with his band of brothers
The Captain sensed new dangers and their plans he'd soon uncover.

The wind delivered whispers as the rumours did increase
No rest could the Captain find, his vexation would not cease
Decisive action was required, a siege, a fight, a war
Gather those still loyal to him and even up the score.

"Your hearts be strong and brave, ye merry sailing crew
Be true to God, keep straight the course, be proud to wear the blue"
These words they sang with bellies full; the Cook's ale sweetly flowed
And fifteen muskets cocked and drawn were ready to explode.

The Captain's men delivered a thunderous killing rain
Of gunshot shells and combat yells while their enemies fell in pain
And those that had the wherewithal to duck the stinging lead
Were quickly found, their hands were bound and they too joined the dead.

Oh shame and woe upon this scene, so bloody and chaotic
And shame upon a spirit mean and a Captain so despotic
And though he'd killed a score of men, his curfew so well timed
The resistant spark was still aglow and no Master could he find.

Further down and further down, into the belly of the boat
The spirit behind the cargo door now exudes a spiteful gloat
The poorly wounded Master crawling down the stairs
The Captain on his knees with a crazy maddening stare.

He knew fate would not be kind and neither would the devil
But there was a conflict for the souls left aboard his vessel
He felt it in the Master who held a blade meant for his throat
He felt it in the evil lurking at the bottom of this boat.

To this day the Captain still searches for the Master
As passing ships avoid The Cross and its deathly dancers

Each night a pair of insane eyes stare into the cargo racks
And something empty, void of feeling stares directly back.

It was in these naked moments that are beyond control
That a terrible understanding was perceived and to this
day unfolds
For the monster in the cargo hold; the cause of all their wrongs
Had been in truth a reflection of their spirits all along.

The Cross's crew forever lost on this ocean of insanity
In its shifting tides of power, possession and vanity
Now cursed to suffer and play their parts for all infinity
Torn between the Cross, it's cargo, the devil and the deep blue sea.

"Whoever fights monsters should see to it that in the process he does not become a monster. And if you gaze long enough into an abyss, the abyss will gaze back into you". **Friedrich Nietzsche.**

(136) I'm Talking To God - 2018 (page 242)

I kneel in a different position each night
Put my hands on the nearest bible
I make a list of all the good things I need
Like living in a universe that's reliable
I've chanted, prayed and searched the faiths
And I think my God will see me right
But he's making it hard for me to hope for the best
Or believe I'll ever see the light
I need comfort and for him to allay my fears?
I'm talking to God but I don't think he wants to hear.

I'm assuming that he's got a plan
And we don't have to suffer an eternity of chaos
I've been towing the line for so long

But I still feel I'm waiting for the pay off
My wealth, health and fortune
Is it down to him, or me, or luck?
Or is the harsh reality
Sometimes things just suck
If he's saying anything then it's not very clear
I'm talking to God but I don't think he wants to hear.

I'm putting up my hand again
I've a got few big questions to ask
I think he's the one that's accountable
And I'm taking him to task
They say you're so great and omnipotent
With your white beard and all
But from where I'm standing
It feels like you dropped a ball
How much more pleading; how many more tears?
I'm talking to God but I don't think he wants to hear.

I was on my knees again last night
Both hands held in prayer
I was clear and my ask heartfelt
But I didn't see any proof you cared
To be perfectly honest
All this imploring is starting to gall
I really don't think you're looking out for me
I'm not sure you're there at all
I bet I'm annoying and you wish I'd disappear
I'm talking to God but I don't think he wants to hear.

I know, I know it's up to me
To provide and support for my family
Stand up tall and do my bit

Control my fear and anxiety
But I thought you were always there in the shadows
And when I was lost you'd guide me home
Over the years I thought I'd felt your presence
But now I think I might have been just alone
It's ok I'll still keep trying to grab your ear
I'm talking to God but I don't think he wants to hear.

(137) Now And What Is Next - 2018 (page 244)

Now

Now is such a temporary condition
Blink and then it's gone
The most important thing you're doing
Is exactly what you've done
It's both monumentally major
And galactically absurd
That anything in any moment
Lasts only as long as this word
Everything gets done NOW
Not sooner or later
Or tomorrow or yesterday
Not some time in the future
Or just nowadays
And when 'now' passes slowly don't be fooled
Just means what you're doing isn't interesting...... that's all.

The sequel ...What Is Next?

Is it something coming that is planned?
Or a mid to premium fashion brand
Does it follow now and then?
Or is it what you're doing next weekend

Perhaps it's the next best thing
Or the next of kin
Is it the next in line?
Or the next good time
Perhaps the girl next door
Or the next World War
I feel so vexed and perplexed
At not knowing
What is next?

(watch out for the follow up "before and after" - if I can be bothered)

(138) Half -2020 (page 245)

It was half time now
And I'd been half asleep
Glass half empty for too long
Half cut and half out of my mind.

I was lying there half naked
Living in a halfway house
On half board
Surviving on half measures.

I was hypnotised by how the other half live
I wasn't going to do things by halves anymore
I knew half a sixpence was better than half a penny
But it was always six of one and half dozen of the other.

Either way it was cheap at half the price
I just needed to be given half a chance
Some people thought I was too clever by half
But they just didn't know the half of it.

(139) The Pursuit Of Happiness - 2021 (page 246)

My pursuit of happiness?
I was hoping to find it in wealth and success
But it's hard to measure what I don't possess
I'm not sure either would have been for the best
Looking back now I'm less impressed

My pursuit of happiness?
I'm always looking forward to a happy ending
But my story arc keeps on changing and bending
It's hard to predict how my fate is trending
Nothing ever seems to end up as I was intending.

My pursuit of happiness?
I wanted to live happily ever after
After the struggle and before the hereafter
Walk into the sunset with joy and laughter
But the rain keeps coming and is falling faster.

My pursuit of happiness?
I've come to know for some, it's the feel of a warm gun
Or Sunday roast with Dad and Mum
Or drinking a Pina Colada in the tropical sun
Or just being a little bit better than everyone.

My pursuit of happiness?
It's the greatest thing that we possess
You can never have too much or an excess
But it's not always easy to recognise or access
And we don't always know when we're well off or blessed
Or having our share of happiness.

(140) The Pursuit Of Happiness Part 2 - 2021 (page 247)

I want a happy house
And a happy family
On a happy path
To getting happy
Living happily ever after
As a happy bunny
Talking happy talk
In a happy valley
I want a happy time
Happy go lucky
In a happy hour
As happy as Larry
I want a happy new year
And a happy holiday
I want many happy returns
On my happy birthday
And a happy Christmas
For everyone
I want shiny happy people
To have fun
I want a happy meal
And a happy coincidence
I want happy pills
After a happy accident
I want to be slap happy
And in my happy place
I want to be trigger happy
Putting on a happy face
As happy as a pig in shit
Or as happy as I can be
And when it comes down to it
I just want to be happy.

"We hold these truths to be self-evident, that all men are created equal, that they are endowed by their Creator with certain unalienable Rights, that among these are Life, Liberty and the pursuit of Happiness."
US Declaration of Independence

(141) T&Cs - 2021 (page 248)

Ralph Lauren and Calvin Klein
Another nickel and another dime
A new deal and an Ace is dealt
By that notable card sharp Franklin D. Roosevelt
They say God's in every flower, hill and dale
But the Devil's always deep in the detail
We've learnt that money never grows on trees
It's all there in the T&Cs.

Jack be nimble and Jack be quick
Jack's going to play his five card trick
He's a player from little Italy
He's a punk who always feels lucky
He'll screw you over given half a chance
He'll blind you with science and put you in a trance
You'll come out worse, that's guaranteed
It's all there in the T&Cs.

Jesus hid out at the Marriott
After shopping Judas Iscariot
He'd been robbing Peter to pay Paul
His loyal disciples, he'd fooled them all
Sleight of hand, a loaf and five fishes
Psalm sixteen and his best wishes
Last seen running across the sea of Galilee
It's all there in the T&Cs.

Condoleezza Rice and Colin Powel
Dick Cheney and Donald Rumsfeld
Well versed in etiquette and obfuscation
And a fruitless search for weapons of negotiation
They want a pact with the United Nations
But all that small print is trying their patience
Where's the evidence that they so dearly need?
It's all there in the T&Cs.

Your life forever subject to approval
By Amazon, Apple, Facebook and Google
Once subscribed they get you purchasing
No surprise your solvency is worsening
It's hard to shop with trust and ease
Laden down with so many consumer policies
And loopholes as old as the Pharisees
It's all there in the T&Cs.

I'm getting tied up in their red tape
The bureaucratic knocks and legal scrapes
The dodgy clauses in invisible ink
Scams, pitches and cunning blueprints
All my shortcuts incur penalties
They've no protection or indemnity
These are now my harsh realities
And it was all there in the T&Cs.

(142) Terribly Alone -2021 (page 249)

On your way to Damascus
Across your very own Rubicon
Clawing out a meaning
From your personal pantheon

Studying the scriptures
The philosophers and scribes
Trying to understand
Why things must fade away and die
If you're living on your own
You might feel terribly alone.

Go have a talk with God
He should answer all your prayers
Maybe your baby
Has got other plans elsewhere
You believe when you fall in love
It's going to be forever
He's fixed a time for you
It's on the twelfth of never
When you bear a heart of stone
You might feel terribly alone.

Beaten up at finishing school
Life's feeling in reverse
Things were getting better
Now they're a whole lot worse
Minutes lonely in your room
With your imaginary friends
In your daydream drama
That you hope will never end
When there's no one on your phone
You might feel terribly alone.

Ask and it will be given to you
Search and you will find
Knock and the door will open
But just not all the time

You've had nothing from the Father
So why not try the son
Who's been dispensing mercy
But just not for everyone
When you feel that hope has flown
You might feel terribly alone.

You might be lost in a supermarket
You might be lost in France
You might be lost at sea
You might be lost in a dance
You might be lost in a dream
You might be lost in the woods
You might be lost in your thoughts
You might be lost for good
When there's no direction home
You might feel terribly alone.

Looking down a black hole
In a far off galaxy
Travelling the universe
For an infinity
Underneath the microscope
Tiny and so pale
Drifting in a magnitude
That's completely off the scale
When you're in the great unknown
You might feel terribly alone.

"Two possibilities exist: either we are alone in the Universe or we are not. Both are equally terrifying." Arthur C Clarke

(143) Time's Fool - 2021 (page 252)

I am time's fool
Losing this daily war of attrition
Time is armed with seconds, minutes, hours and days
I've got none of that ammunition
If I could turn back time,
Through cosmetic surgery
Then I would drive straight to Harley Street
To secure my immortality
I am time's fool
And under his sickle I will be dispatched
Physically fading away
Against time I am no match
Time can be a jet plane
Or not move like a rock
Time will take away everything
But in the end, time is all we've got
Time resolves heartache
Bereavement and grief
Time brings solace to the poor
And for the sick, relief
Time can dissolve mountains
And build towns
Time can raise up kings
Then time can tear them down
Time never stops it's relentless crawl
Sometime, anytime or no time at all
I'm locked in time with no chance of withdrawal
I can't escape through a time tunnel.

I am time's fool
Hoping diet and exercise
Will stave off its drive

To plot my demise
I try and do ten things at once
So I have more time in the day
But I get distracted
And let time slip away
Time used to be kinder to me
When I was young, free and able
But here I lay prostrate
Getting eroded on time's table
I try and fight time
I'm one of mortality's soldiers
But each day I lose some ground
And get a little older
We might have peace in our time
Or we might have war
But time doesn't care
What we're fighting or not fighting for
Yes, all the time in this universe
Infinitely bends and curls
But we're idiots to think
We have all the time in the world
And when we say sorry for your loss
At time of death
That's because time has deserted us
And there's no time left
I'm time's fool
Of that there is no doubt
And in my brief hours and weeks
Time will win and wipe me out.

"Love's not Time's fool, though rosy lips and cheeks
Within his bending sickle's compass come"
Sonnet 116 William Shakespeare.

(144) When Did We Stop Believing In God -2022 (page 254)

When did we stop believing in God?
Was it the time the first sun god failed to make the sun shine
Or when we realised we knew a lot more than Apollo
Or when we were no longer so enamoured with Odin and Thor
Because we had more fashionable deities we could follow
Was it when we no longer feared or were in awe
Of the havoc God threatened to wreak on the world
Because no matter what was predicted in the book of revelations
We could just as easily do it ourselves
God used to be both magical and omnipotent
Until Science and God had a head on collision
And God never put forward an alternative narrative
Was it then we started losing our religion?
When did we realise much to our disappointment and surprise
There wasn't really much need to keep faith and behave
As just doing good deeds and living a good life
Didn't guarantee our fortune or in the end we'd be saved
For centuries we have tried to find God
Inwardly, outwardly or from observing the universe through the Hubble
At what point did we consider our search might never pay off
And theologically speaking we may be in trouble
How could someone so loving and divine
In whose name our children we happily anoint
Could sacrifice the life of his one and only son
Just to teach us a lesson and prove a point
If he's really walking by our side
All the way from here until infinity
Why then does he sanction so much chaos and misery
With a vague but plausible deniability.

When did we stop believing in God?
Was it 1906 when he lost his heavenly glow

After the earthquake in San Francisco
Or following Belsen and Nagasaki
Or after the 2011 Japanese Tsunami
Was it during the Black Death and the Great Plague
Or was it 9/11 when we became disengaged
And what do we believe in now?
Following decades of mistrust and superstition
Is it in......
Consequence unfettered of conscience
Driven by powerful need and greed
In ever decreasing circles of obsession
To gain, acquire and commercially succeed
Is it in......
Gaslighted strongly held opinions
Without foundation or proof
Titbits of spin and rumour
Which are sexier than the truth
Hell and heaven aren't the places of interest they used to be
They've lost their enigma and standing
We don't believe anyone is going to really get judged or punished
For going to war or their borders expanding
But ....
There are new threats casting shadows
Inducing panic and worrying bouts
Our recent self righteousness and confidence
Has been replaced with foreboding and self doubt.

It has been said, in some quarters, God is only a concept
By which we measure our pain
But our lack of belief and disdain
May in its place, leave a space
For self interest and chaos to reign
It might be time to start believing in something again.

(145) Definition Of Done - 2022 (page 256)

What's the definition of done?
Does it mean finished and complete
Over and done?
Is it done and dusted
Or no sooner said than done?
Perhaps it's a done deal
Where no harms done
Is it easier said than done
Or well done
And ok if it's over done
Or under done
Or done to a crisp?
What about if you're hard done by
Is that your just desserts?
Or does it mean you've been there, done that and got the tshirt
Have you done to others
What they don't want done to them?
Are things done all the time
Or just now and then?
And when you say you're done in
That might not be entirely true
Because I don't think you can say you're done
Until you've had something done to you.

I heard someone done a runner
And isn't coming back
He went from Lands End to Dunfermline
Now staying at Dunroamin
And moaning
And not done yet
He shouldn't have done it.

Sometimes there so much to do
Or nothing's getting done
Which can leave you glum
But worse if you're a woman
As their work is never done
There's nothing you can do that can't be done
It has been said
But does doing nothing mean
Things are undone instead
Does the very act of doing
Mean you've done something
Or is it really like Stevie said
'You haven't done nuthin"
Is done done when you reach the top
And if we don't know what done is
How will we know where to stop?
Is done done when we reach the summit
And do we ever really know who's done it.

(I'm pleased that's done now).

Age And Passing

(146) Falling Away- 2001 (page 259)

She went to bed with an Ovaltine and awoke still in a dream
Strolling in a foggy drizzle by a cloudy stream
The who or what escapes her
The why has long since passed
Her memories are selective and fading fast.

She's falling away
The lights are on but the residents may have gone
She's falling away
Too often the kids find she's not always home.

Her beautiful idiosyncrasies
Are losing their once resilient chemistry
Her days drift by like smoke rings dissolving in the air
We've tried to get close to her but she's not always there.

She's falling away
Her hands are not the trusted companions they used to be
She's falling away
Degenerative headwinds blowing at her constantly.

Sometimes things are too bright, other times sepia grey
The minutes pass so slowly but the hours are slipping away
She's a reluctant passenger and she travels all alone
To a deserted destination and she won't be coming home.

She's falling away
When we're together she's often somewhere else
She's falling away
Falling away from everything, including herself.

(147) I Never Expected To See - 2001 (page 260)

I never expected to see
The fading of my agility
I never expected to be
This person staring back at me
I never expected to hear
My Mother forget my name
I never expected to suffer
With back pain
I never expected to greet
An old friend with not much hair
I never expected to meet
A young man offering me a chair
I never expected a time
When I could see my end in sight
I never expected I'd rely on someone else
To turn out the light.

Recently I've reflected
It was all a whole lot worse than I expected.

(148) Taking Just One More Breath - 2005 (page 260)

Taking just one more breath
That wafer thin line between life and death
The sad difference between going and gone
As dark clouds gather and the night moves inexorably along
One final task, one more test
Taking just one more breath.

Taking just one more breath
As the mourners watch and the tears dry
There's nothing left to do or hide

The cool breeze of night's gentle caress
Be still now and be blessed
Taking just one more breath.

Taking just one more breath
As the shroud of emptiness covers the ward
As the last strands are cut from the cord
The fluorescent lights flicker and wane
As the albino attendant clears up again
The wafer thin line between awake and rest
Taking just one more breath.

(149) Precious Sand - 2006 (page 261)

Part 1

Sand
Never used to bother me
But it does now
The sand that used to trickle
Is pouring through the hourglass
My eggs are nearly done!
I'm slowly being sanded down
Lost in sandalwood
Living in a sand castle,
Eating my sandwiches
Reading my sandpaper
Listening to Sandy Shaw's "Puppet on a string"
In my sandals.

There's sand everywhere
Sand in the desert
Sand by the sea
Sand in our buildings

Sand in the bags that prevent the flooding to our homes and communities.

There's precious sand in the stained glass windows
Precious memories of sand between my toes
I suggest we enjoy life as much as we can
Before our hourglasses drain of sand.

Part 2

The things that sand us down

- the shackles of ambition
- the cares of adulthood
- the fear of uncertainty
- the show and the mask
- the chore and the task
- the deadlines to deliver
- being provider and giver
- the middle of the night shiver.

(150) Darkest Dark - 2006 (page 262)

The dead heat of the night
Drifts through the open window pane
Curtains are pulled, blinds are shut
The sun might not shine again
The odd light flickers
Hoping dawn will join its fight
I can feel the walls closing in
In the darkest dark
Of the darkest night.

My skin crawls, time crawls
Like a paralysed last breath

The slow march of the inexorable
The cavalcade of death
The leading players play their parts
Grief is a parasite
Feeding on the saddest souls
In the darkest dark
Of the darkest night.

The pit of loneliness
Before the birds begin their singing
My heart beats too fast
An uncaring silence is ringing
I dreamt of a horse drawn carriage
But it offered no comfort or respite
I lay awake and can't sleep right
In the darkest dark
Of the darkest night.

(151) I Think I'm Ready Now -2008 (page 263)

When the day is long but the sun won't rise
When my stack of worries reaches my eyes
When nothing any more is ever a surprise
When I'm lost in a multitude of lies.

When all I hear are angry growls
Then I think I'm ready now.

I've been Father, lover, husband and son
It took me a long time to know I'm not the same as everyone
It took me a long time to find my voice and the song I've since sung
It was only then I understood the web I'd spun.

I need to be somewhere, somehow

I think I'm ready now.

I've seen the crescent of the moon in the darkness of the night
I've seen good men lose before a fight
I've been wrong even when I was right
I've opened my mouth when I should have shut it tight.

Let me take just one more bow
I think I'm ready now.

I used to care but not anymore
I don't dress up like I did before
It's your turn to hold open the door
I don't track, chase or keep score.

I've wiped the fears from my furrowed brow
I think I'm ready now.

It's your turn to lead not mine
I can't be concerned if you don't feel fine
It's your clock ticking and not on my time
They're your ties now to bind.

It's your field to care for and to plough
I think I'm ready now.

(152) The Half Light 2013 (page 264)

I can feel the shadows closing in
Twilight's sad kiss before it welcomes the night
Just for a moment I was lost in time
Listening to "Drowning by numbers"
The day, a memory now; seeped in melancholy and an unfulfilled yearning
Now servant to reflection and sepia grey reverie

The old rocking chair is still in the corner
A kind old hand upon my shoulder
Then for a fleeting second
I'm walking again across the arc of my highlands
Surveying the past vistas and undulations
Unravelling in time and piling up
All that vast spread of people and things
A sigh before I ascend again
And turn to welcome the shadows of the half light.

(153) Winter Is Coming - 2014 (page 265)

I realised too late in Autumn
I hadn't always been myself
The voice I'd acquired, had none of my fire
And sounded like everyone else
It wasn't the best reflection of me
Autumn was here much too quickly.

When it was Spring I was afraid to sing
When it was Summer I hid behind Mother
And I wouldn't dare interrupt her
Now at times, there are warning signs
Of crackling frosts and Auld Lang Syne
Simmering soup and creaking chairs
And faltering voices beyond repair
I spent too long trying to discover
My place in the fretful Spring and Summer
I spent too long feeling doubtful
In my own confident counsel
And now that I have the courage to speak freely
I fear it will leave me
Like the Autumn leaves
That fall too quickly.

Winter is coming ...as Jon Snow knows
There aren't many weeks left to go
So while I can, I'll sing my heart out
Through all of Winter's coldest bouts
I'll stand and resist
Until 1 cease To exist
Even when I'm dried up, bent and crawling
Selfish, infirm and bawling
Telling anyone that cares to come calling
That I will not rest
Whilst I contest my Summer spent stalling.

(154) Grey Area - 2018 (page 266)

Unsatisfying
On the fence
Try to cover it up
But it's just a pretence
Unedifying
A sign of approaching old age
Of the weak and selfish brigade
Shades of ...
Well that just isn't an answer
50 shades of.....
And you're a sado-masochistic ballroom dancer
It's the unsexy place
Where judgements are made.
It's the space between wrong and right
Or black and white
Day and night
Salt and pepper
Or now or never
It's compromise

The colour of the vacant
Distant and hypnotised.

All this chatter?
Could be a figment of my grey matter.

(155) Porcupine - 2019 (page 267)

Say hello to varicose veins
And arthritic aches and pains
Don't worry keep time
I want to be a porcupine.

Say goodbye to serious dating
I wonder who we're next cremating?
Don't hurry, read the signs
I want to be a porcupine.

Cooking something when I get home
Going to eat it all alone
I accept it and don't whine
I want to be a porcupine.

I'm a prick and I'm a pain
Always looking for someone to blame
Going forward but left behind
I want to be a porcupine.

Pins, needles and prickly spines
Get to close and I'll make you cry
Not sorry, I'm unkind
I want to be a porcupine.

I get the jobs no else one will do

Just tell me who you need me to screw
It's tragic, but I'm fine
I want to be a porcupine.

(156) I'm Closing Down - 2019 (page 268)

I'm closing down
Bolting the door
Sweeping the floor
Taking the displays off the ground
Putting up the closing signs
Selling everything at a markdown
I'm closing down.

I'm closing down
Packing my case
Leaving this town
Having one last look around
"You've all been like family to me
I've got many happy memories
Of the first day the doors opened"
But now they are closed and broken
I'm closing down.

I'm closing down
I've traded long enough
Selling all sorts of stuff
Some of it crap
Some of it tack
Some of it half decent
Some of it came back
Nothing left to put on the shelf or racks
I'm closing down.

I'm closing down
Taking the business offline
Going underground
Reconciling the ledger
Balancing the books
Paying off the debts
Writing the last cheques
I'm closing down.

I'm closing down
Writing the closing speech
Choosing the exit music
We say we'll stay in contact
But I don't hold out for that
And if we do
It will be like ghosts of friends we once knew
Everything now has gone for a burton
It's curtains
I'm closing down.

(157) Stay With Me - 2019 (page 269)

She put coffee on an old distressed stove
An Autumn breeze blowing across her face
Her daughter laughing with a lady from down the lane
Whilst putting fresh flowers into a vase
The smell of pastries and newly baked bread
Prepared by the baker's wife
Sun cutting through the moving clouds
Dogs trotting by excited and wild
What more to hear and see?
Stay with me?

Rain was forecast but it was just a small shower

As the church bell chimed at the 11th hour
This morning we walked, shopped and browsed
Picking up fruit and buying some cake
We said good morning to a passing friend
Then stopped to take a break
I leaned back in the cushioned chair
Whilst reading the paper I check you're still there
You look sad, full of melancholy
Stay with me?

Later in the day we visit a local church
Ask ourselves why we haven't done this before?
Marvel at the beams and spires
The shaded marble and stained glass panes
A service hushes our whispered conversation
We donate a pound and light a candle
Neatly step across the buried bones
Together, but we're alone
Under the domes of this heavenly canopy
Stay with me?

(158) He Knows The Score - 2020 (page 270)

The minutes are passing
Time is getting tighter
The prognosis isn't great
But he's a fighter
He's slipped into
A vortex of doubt
It's not now about resilience
Or punching his way out
All of the numbers
Don't make sense anymore
It doesn't matter who's winning now

He knows the score.

He gets frustrated
And hates feeling bad
He regrets not using
All the charm he once had
This swollen river
Will lap at his feet
It'll just keep flowing
Way past to his seat
He wanted to endure
Be the last out of the door
But it doesn't matter who's winning now
He knows the score.

The room is swaying
He's tied to his chair
Nothing to do
And he's not going anywhere
He once held dominion
In the land of the free
But now just a stranger
In a strange country
And getting up is such a chore
It doesn't matter who's winning now
He knows the score.

In the white heat of the night
He begs for an answer
He needs a magician or wizard
Or a necromancer
He's going down to the bottom
He'll submerge on his own

He's got nothing but affection
For all the friends he's known
He's over regret
But it still feels raw
It doesn't matter who's winning now
He knows the score.

(159) Ill Feelings - After The Wake - 2021 (page 272)

The room was still
There was nothing else to say
Just the gentle rhythm of the heating
And the pitter patter of drizzle
On the window pane.

The phones had been silenced
Notifications turned to silent
The tables have been cleared
The players are now all quiet.

The funny stories and anecdotes
Now finished and applauded
No more sad reflections
No more showering his name
With plaudits.

And no more tears to shed
Just the cards to place around the room
The flowers to water
And the slow long walk to bed.

Alone here in the dark
A pale lunar glow
Creeps through the curtains

Like a searchlight on the ceiling
It's the moon and these ill feelings.

(160) Sleep Or Adjust? - 2021 (page 273)

The tinnitus, the aching, the fading and the waning
The greying strands of hair reflected in the mirror
The years of repetitive strain, now an irritating pain
We wish our pool of memories could be clearer
But we know
We all have to go
And become one with the dust
So should we sleep or adjust?

Daily we feel sadder as we struggle with our bladders
We're not the young guns we were once in the past
More trips to the physician, to help manage our conditions
We worry how much longer we can last
But we know
And it's all starting to show
We'll waste away, we'll rust
So should we sleep or adjust?

We treat the young with derision because we've got tunnel vision
We're obscured by the fog of benign cataracts
We prefer music from the past and think today's is really daft
We spy from our front windows, while the neighbours watch our back
But we know
When we're feeling low
It's in God we trust
So should we sleep or adjust?

There is no amazing grace, a fact we have to face
That can save the shrivelled wrecks we have become

Selfish self absorbed, we mean nothing untoward
We're just poor losers in the race that's never won
But we know
Through life's highs and lows
Fate is unjust
So should we sleep or adjust?

Our children used to adore us
They'd never say you "bore us"
We hit the high notes in each chorus
We were proud like a Tyrannosaurus
Respected like The Walrus
Shone like an Aureus
From Havana to Honduras
Our anecdotes uproarious
Our early years victorious
Everyone was for us
But now they just ignore us
Or worse they must deplore us
Because our behaviour is notorious
Both unpleasant and inglorious
And never meritorious
And life is now just so...
.....laborious.

Our days are getting longer as the seconds tick away
But the sun and moon dash daily across the sky
Each evening we ascend by the stairlift once again
To bedrooms plain and cold and old and dry
But we know
We're getting slow
But if we stop we're stuffed
So should we sleep or adjust?

(161) I Just Can't Get The Ending Right - 2021 (page 275)

My plot thickens, meanders and twists
Jumps from revelation to surprise
I can just about sustain
All those unbelievable narrative ties
My story has got hooks, it's got pace, and some profound truth
Some lines excite and some raise the roof
But no matter how hard I try into the fading light
I just can't get the ending right.

She was sweet, she was kind
She had great big round opal eyes
Here she was with me tonight
Things were going well I surmised
I'd made every effort to get thing's right
If I could sparkle then things might ignite
And I might be someone she'd grow to like
But by dessert she had taken flight
I just can't get the ending right.

I always thought that I was singled out
To enjoy a brilliant career
If things didn't work out as predicted
I'd still be ahead of my peers
I've been in many random roles
With various vacuous goals
Some well led and some out of control
But now I'm older, disillusioned and less bright
And I just can't get the ending right.

The nurse comes in and adjusts my chair
Opens the blind and tops up my water
She takes my pulse and combs my hair

I'm expecting a visit from my daughter
Where are the tributes, the choirs and the flowers?
Didn't I have a life and didn't I once have power?
I never expected I'd whimper off at the eleventh hour
And fade gently into the night
But I don't have the strength to put up another fight
I just can't get the ending right.

(162) Looking At An Old Photograph - 2022 (page 276)

I was looking at an old photograph
Listening to "Seven Days Walking" by Ludovico Einnaudi
It was of a past Christmas Day
The table was laid
And Mum smiled proudly
I could just about see our old TV
A Christmas special on the BBC
Top of the Pops or Eric and Earnie?
And nestling under the tree
All the presents laid out for the family
How could I have possibly known
Of the gifts we shared that day
None would have the depth and beauty
Of this old photo I'm looking at today.

(163) She Wandered In Dreams - 2022 (page 276)

She wandered in dreams for the last time
Her eyes flickered and trembled
To the rhythmic thrum of the ventilator hum
Her drugs neatly assembled
Her laboured breathing and pale visage
And intermittent moans of pain
Between her delirious mumblings

And her requests for water again.

She wandered in dreams for the last time
Where it was no one can say
Perhaps she's sailing on a deep blue sea
On a glorious summer's day
With exotic booze on a luxury cruise
In a time that's not today
And not recall a fate so cruel
That is set to take her away.

She wandered in dreams for the last time
We hope in a fond location
Far away from this parade
Of sadness and suffocation
Where she can fly across the sky
Or stand upright and feel strong
Not burdened by these deathly ties
In a life she can't prolong.

She wandered in dreams for the last time
Did a tear roll down her cheek?
Has she resigned to say goodbye?
Though she can hardly speak
When her dream is over
And she has no need of sleep
She'll go her way accordingly
We'll bow our heads and weep.

(164) When I Didn't Care - 2020 (page 277)

When I was a little boy
It felt like the world was created just for me
I was kind of prince of everything

Including my anxieties
Things were so much easier when I didn't care.

I could be cruel, I could be kind
I was my own grand design
I even got unprompted smiles from random strangers
I cut up worms, ingested germs
Ignored the lessons I was meant to learn
I had no concept of danger.

I was such a carefree soul
Gliding everywhere
Things were so much easier when I didn't care.

Bouncing around my bedroom
Feeling three sheets to the wind
My Hi-Fi turned up to maximum
Ignoring complaints about the din
Things were so much easier when I didn't care.

I could be rash, I could be brash
I could be charming in a flash
I was the great entertainer
I would be rude and sometimes crude
I didn't mind whose ear I chewed
Proud of getting off with strangers.

I was so ridiculous
But just a joke I swear
Things were so much easier when I didn't care.

Alcohol and an overdraft
Was all I thought I'd need

I'd happily take anything
Except maybe taking heed
Things were so much easier when I didn't care.

I was the King with half a crown
Until the bills came around
I thought I was on a great retainer
With weekend holidays
To Amsterdam for the day
Or getting away in a manger.

Money wasn't everything
As long as I had my share
Things were so much easier when I didn't care.

I didn't keep an eye on anything
I didn't do things by stealth
I was really alright physically
Not worried about mental health
Things were so much easier when I didn't care.

I could be smashed, paralytic
Next day coherent, energetic
I might get bruised but nothing major
I would eat this and eat that
Mostly saturated fat
I now owe my body so many favours.

The chickens have come home to roost
And I'm beyond repair
Things were so much easier when I didn't care.

Relationships were simple then

It was just with me and me
No desire at that point
To start a family
Things were so much easier when I didn't care.

I was obtuse, on the loose
There was no good excuse
For my poor behaviour
When she left I must confess
I guess it was for the best
I couldn't blame her.

I had it all, just for myself
In a life I wouldn't share
Things were so much easier when I didn't care.

Now my head is in my hands
Trying to keep all my troubles in
So many things to care about
I just don't know where to begin
Things were so much easier when I didn't care

Am I heading for another crash
When will fate and I next clash?
There just seem to be so many dangers
My life has become so chaotic
I've veered from calm to psychotic
In the mirror a worn out stranger.

I guess it's nothing sinister
But it's coming at me everywhere
Things were so much easier when I didn't care

But I care now, it's true- I really do.

(165) I Can Still Smell Everything - 2022 (page 281)

I can't see so well
My eyesight's got progressively worse
I can't hear so well
I sometimes struggle to converse
I miss the doorbell when it rings
And can't see all that's happening
I don't have a clue what tomorrow will bring
...... but I can still smell everything.

I can smell every rat and rodent
I wake up early and smell the coffee
I know what won't come up smelling of roses
Or smells suspiciously dodgy.

I can smell trouble coming
Or something past its date of expiry
I know the smell of napalm in the morning
And that's another smell entirely.

Some people I smell a mile off
With deals too good to be true
I can smell when they're talking bullshit
And the rhetorical crap they spew.

I know when something smells off
Full of garbage and incompetence
I can sniff out all sorts of aromas
But I wish more were common scents.

I've known the sweet smell of success

Or when something stinks like hell
There isn't much I can really rely on
Accept my sense of smell.

(166) My Last Time Up The Junction -2023 (page 282)

(in the key of E Major)

It happened again in Streatham
Another drinking session
This recovering alcoholic
Still loves a gin and tonic
My doctor often warned me
To take the meds he bought me
My liver is a real mess
So why am I still legless?

I never see my daughter
She's living in Gibraltar
Her husband's in the army
A squaddie born in Barnsley
Her Mother's a lot older
She's now divorced the soldier
Our memories in a folder
I wish that I could hold her.

I still visit my mate Stanley
Though he can't understand me
He gets washed over by the nurses
In a care home which he curses
He's suffering with dementia
And can't eat without his dentures
He swears at passing strangers

He has very strange behaviours.

(Middle eight)

It wasn't very clever
Not trying to get better
So before the pain got too horrific
I rushed off to the clinic
They made me an appointment
Which was a disappointment
To see a heart consultant
Down in deepest Holborn.

(in the key of D Major)

This evening at 6.50
They strapped me rather nifty
To a defibrillator
Where 15 minutes later
I was put on to a stretcher
I had very high blood pressure
All much to my displeasure
A moment I won't treasure.

(back to E Major)

And now I must be patient
For my urgent operation
I'm going to need a surgeon
The prognosis is uncertain
I'm registered as high risk
Dependent on the chair lift
I can't control when I piss

All I do is exist.

The truth is in me sinking
I spent too much time just drinking
It's something that I can't duck
Things are really screwed up
My life has been a car crash
This is now the backlash
So now it's my deduction
It's my last time up the junction.

Thank you Difford & Tilbrook!!

(167) This Much Is True - 2022 (page 284)

Put away your speeches and your company car
Say goodbye to flip charts and performance bars
One last annual Summer yachting cruise
There's already someone here to fill your shoes
Who can bite off all the things you now can't chew
The minutes of the meeting aren't yours now to review.

Every flower you've tended, every tree you've grown
Every weed you've cut and every seed you've sown
Has led you to this garden you now frequent
Recalling all the things you're owed and all you've spent
The lawyers in the chambers await their cue
It's time to make your peace and pay your dues.

The dizzying sickening aura of your stained glass pane
All the lightning flashes of your disdain
Seasick apparitions haunt your past
They are setting sail now at half mast
One last time to stand and inspect your crew

The Mayflower sails tonight but not with you.

The sky is getting greyer and the ground is cold
All your second features are looking old
The solitary magpie on your roof
Has come with one for sorrow and two for truth
You've got nothing left to share, no points of view
The case for change isn't yours now to approve.

Finish that last seance you have to conduct
Then you can collect your blanket and fill up your cup
Put away your joke books and your puns
It's time to set the phasers all to stun
No more affirmations to pursue
The game is up, the cards aren't yours to choose.

No more royal assignments, you're all done with them
No more court positions with strange acronyms
The brass band that was marching to your beat
Will no longer play your tune, it's obsolete
You've just one more appointment and rendezvous
Your passing out parade and farewell do.

Cut down your holly and your Christmas Tree
They're just so out of line in this cold February
The withered reef that's hanging from your door
Has no real purpose anymore
One last hymn to sing in the church pew
A host of golden angels have left your retinue.

Your days are getting shorter as your room gets dark
You've run out of the time you had to make your mark
You're feeling old and oh so very tired

Your best before date has long since expired
The phones are set to silent just for you
It's time for you to leave, this much is true.

The Covid Climate War Poems

(168) The Whispering Gallery - 2019 (page 288)

Ok I know the score, you don't need to whisper anymore
Ok I know what's up, don't be shy please speak up
Ok I've got the time, just tell me what's on your mind.

So why send me...?
Little tributaries of tittle tattle
Half caught shadows of conversation
It could be this, it might be that?
Vapid smoke of indistinct meaning
Of lost ill judged gaslighted opinions
Words dashing across the digital highway
Or lost or stuck in a verbal byway
From anodyne to philistine
An annoying whine
Null and void
From hateful to paranoid.

Why couldn't you just call it out?
But there you are whispering, whispering
Something trite and condescending
Hollow platitudes that aren't worth defending
White lies and indiscriminate venting
So much dissenting, meddling and bending
Is it all worth all this trending, posturing and pretending?

I can handle the truth
After all it's not the end of the world ….is it?

(169) The Kingdom Falling Down - 2020 (page 288)

Late December 2019

First sign of trouble and what might be coming
We should have breathed deeply
While we still had time to prepare
When we weren't reliant on ventilators and intensive care
We had never heard of Hubei or Wuhan until then
Where they say you can get anything my friend
Bats, lizards, fever or shortness of breath
Or unforeseen premature death
Then from the streets of Rome to Milan
Had to keep your distance and wash your hands
No one needed to be courageous
We just had to avoid being contagious
Hang on to your pots of gold
Look after your toilet rolls
Can you hear it? - can you hear that sound
It's the Kingdom falling down.

It's the end of the world as we know it
But we don't feel fine
We've been daydream believers of the worse kind
I used to look forward to holding your hand
But now I'm just a nowhere man
If music be the food of love
Better learn how to stream it bruv
See that red door - they'll need to paint it black
No more hitting the road Jack
They're not jive talking or telling us lies
So I'm going to focus on staying alive
If I'm outside leave me alone
When I'm inside I'm at home
I know exactly where I've been
I've been out of my brain social distancing
Can you hear it? - in your hometown

It's the Kingdom falling down.

Worst disaster since the second world war
A world crisis that started in Chinese Manchuria
Next to Italy and then to Spain
Where tyrants were taking control again
Insipid response from the League of Nations
No member state making the necessary preparations
People thrown to the wolves in the ensuing melee
Abandoned soldiers left to fight the bloody fray
From Paris to the bay of Dunkirk
From Stalingrad to the Egyptian desert
While the USA stayed in its transatlantic nest
Slave to politicians and its self interest
Eighty one years this September
To recall the lessons we should have tried to remember
Can you hear it? - it's all around
It's the Kingdom falling down.

We had all the freedom, coffee and pills
Virgin Atlantic and digital thrills
Our civil rights, our cause des celebres
All our debts on the never - never
We ignored the portents but believed the absurd
Then sold our souls to Mark Zuckerburg
We tore down Camelot and now it's gone
Replaced it with a self serving Babylon
We keenly click on Sodom and Gomorrah
We're indifferent to porn and horror
We burn fuel and watch the world boil
But now you can't get jack for a litre of oil
It's a mirror reflecting our true nature
Cracking like an overheated glacier

Can you hear it?- the glass shattering on the ground
It's the Kingdom falling down.

I've been trying to preserve my mental health
I'm going to have a Great Depression all by myself
I'm like Bill Murray or Punxatony Phil
Every day I wake up and check I'm not ill
Caught in a landslide, no escape from reality
I won't walk on the wild side so don't stand so close me
Is this how it ends with a whimper not a bang
All my plans, well I guess they can all go hang
Walking up and down Escher's stairs
No surprise I'm not getting anywhere
No more trips to Sugar Town
All my stock value heading down
There must be some way out of here?
That lets me protect the things I hold dear
Can you hear it? - listen don't make a sound
It's the Kingdom falling down.

We should play those old 33s
Put on those faded CDs
Let's listen to "La Traviata"
And Beethoven's "Moonlight Sonata"
"Songs For Swingin Lovers" by Frank Sinatra
Leonard Cohen's "You Want It Darker"
"Highway 61" and "Highway To Hell"
Rossini's overture "William Tell"
"Revolver" and "Rubber Soul"
The Rolling Stones "It's only Rock and Roll"
Leonard Bernstein and Bernard Herrmann
"On The Town" and "Torn Curtain"
Stevie Wonder and FleetWood Mac

"Don't Let Me Down" and "Get Back"
Surf's up as well I hear you shout
Something to play for a wipe out
Can you hear it Johnny? - going round and round
It's the Kingdom falling down.

This is when the earth stood really still
No CGI needed to make it feel real
We hid beneath the planet of the apes
And are still planning our great escape
Hoping for our independence day
Or a superhero to take our troubles away
It's like the War of the Worlds
Without Orson Welles
And without a shadow of a doubt
No one can leave or get out
It's the night of the living dead
Wearing our surgical masks in bed
It's apocalypse now and death's dark caress
All the way to the heart of darkness
I'll follow the script and I promise I'll behave
Just don't leave me in a shallow grave
Can you see it? - the movie coming to town
It's the Kingdom falling down.

The hard truth is
Some of our elected leaders just aren't up to this
We've made our bed and now we've got to lie in it
We anticipate our early evening briefing
And the measured ministerial greeting
Hearing about the trend lines and the spikes
And an apology for the science not being precise
Getting an update on PPE

And the cold logic of herd immunity
The drop in share price and GDP
And making sacrifices for our country
We'll need the best strategists and brains
This won't be like the Apprentice or running a hotel chain
Your luck ran out my friend some time ago
Just saying your plan is beautiful won't make it so
We've got an awfully long way to go
So spare us the unnecessary disappointment and distress
Don't tell us this will be over by Christmas
Can you hear it? - listen gather round
It's the Kingdom falling down.

This could be your last time on the planet
Your last night on earth
Your last minute in the whole universe
Your last day between now and your birth
The last thing you do for all it's worth
The last time to play the Beatles and the Stones
The last time to use your mobile phone
The last time to have a vodka on the rocks
The last time to rock around the clock
Hush hush whisper who dares
Who's that in the shadows saying their prayers?
Is it Cordelia and mad King Lear?
And the ghostly figures of some well known financiers
They turn to the audience stage right
Share their soliloquies and vanish into the night
They are still out there performing
Those villains, fools and clowns
In a brand new show playing in town
It's the Kingdom falling down.

"Tis the times' plague, when madmen lead the blind."
— William Shakespeare, King Lear.

(170) Straightforward Again - 2020 (page 294)

Well she danced on the path
As we heard the blocks tumbling
Her brother had crashed
Into the tower she'd made
The sky was so dark
Full of grey clouds and thunder
Her mother indoors
Sipping warm lucozade.

There's no obvious reason and no one's to blame
But nothing will be straightforward again.

The last time we went
To our local theatre
We smiled and we laughed
So excitedly
We went to the park
Bought coffee and pastries
The days were getting longer
New buds on the trees.

Perhaps things will improve or it's worse than they claim
But nothing will be straightforward again.

He woke in the night
Feeling under the weather
Was it a cough or a cold?
Or a slight touch of fever
It seemed far too long

Since he last hugged his mother
The daffodils bloomed
And the football was on.

They'll still be sunshine and they'll still be rain
But nothing will be straightforward again.

They say things will get worse
Before they get better
We must be observant
Together alone
We pray for the days
When the shops are all open
The parks are all full
And we can leave home.

Things feel the same and perhaps not much has changed
But nothing will be straightforward again

I don't want to appear mournful
But I think it's the end of normal.

(171) Pale White Lies - 2020 (page 295)

They say we are winning the war
But we just can't beat the disease
They massage the kill count numbers
Of the sick and the north communist Vietnamese
Descent at the democratic convention
Marches on Lincoln Park
Flowers in the rifle muzzles
Of the National Guard
We're told once more how well we're doing
As the test data is unveiled

But the leaders all look haunted
Another white lie turns a shade of pale.

Mama San died in a care home
Mama Cass died shortly too
They both took hydroxychloroquine
Because he'd told them to
The facts were hard to swallow
We could never hold the hill
Dying in the elephant grass
Expecting air cover or a pill
And so it was that later
As the anchor man told his tale
Another massacre at tea time
Another white lie turns a shade of pale.

At the presidential briefing
He said stop the locking down
So they opened up the churches
The high streets and the towns
But there was a cover up in My Lai
And a corden around New York
We could hear the rolling thunder
But no one was prepared to talk
They shot students in Ohio
And bombed the Ho Chi Minh trail
And they call this the scent of victory
Another white lie turns a shade of pale.

He loved the smell of napalm
And the inside of a mask
The feel of a protective apron
And an M16's blast

He'd volunteered for the front line
As soon as his draft card came through
But was he killing or saving?
We really didn't have a clue
On Thursday he was front page
By Friday the news was stale
We said we'd be there for him
Another white lie turns a shade of pale.

The Vietnam war, which lasted from 1955 to 1975, resulted in the deaths of 58,220Americans. COVID-19 surpassed that number in less than four months.

(172) Goldfish Bowl - 2020 (page 297)

By the time it happened....
He thought he was on the last rung
Of a ladder that was never that tall
He looks over his dominion
Which is pretty small
A couple of saving accounts
Garden out the back
A mortgage free house
Three married kids and neighbours with a cat
How did he get here?
Where had he been?
No great mystery
Or dramatic arcs or themes
Now holed up and shut down
Working from home
Just the hum of his laptop's cooling system
To remind me him he's not alone
He counts the hours, watches the time
Thinks about ordering something on Prime

He rarely changes the clothes he's worn
He likes to track the growth of his lawn
There are lots of new things he hasn't done before
Like making lists and pasting them to the kitchen door
He worries that his mental health isn't feeling so bright
He gets regular offers to put it right
He feels like he's waiting to be prorogued?
Or furloughed or something like that
He waves again to the neighbour's cat
He feels like a nowhere man
Living in a little box land
He doesn't have any plans
To go out or get dressed
He worries he's getting careless
He feels he's starting to care less
Perhaps they'll put him in a care home
He doesn't want to live out the rest of his life in monochrome
Last night he drank too much wine
Today he's not feeling so fine
He thinks the neighbour's cat is overfed
He should race that cat to bed
Is there Formica all around
Or is it in his head?
Oh brother you guessed
He's under house arrest
Feeling like he's trapped
In a personal submersible
In isolated water
Since the restraining order.

He used to be a hopeless romantic
Now he's a hopeless soul
Wading at the bottom

Of a deep dank double glazed hole
He used to be so very special
Always treated like a guest
Now he's the same as everyone else
Antisocially self obsessed
He needs to give up worrying
About the things he can't control
Like nextdoor's cat
And living in a goldfish bowl.

(173) Anymore - 2020 (page 299)

I'm not so sure
Anymore
I'm not so sure
I never saw the warning signs
Now I'm running out of time.

When you told me that you'd reached the end
There was nowhere else you could hide
Your family was falling apart
It was tearing you up inside
Your brother and sister at each other's throats
Saying things that should never have been said
Their parents felt they had let them down
Things were really coming to a head.

We're not so sure
Anymore
We're not so sure
Everyone can sink just a little more
Until they're crawling across the floor.

I meant to spend all day feeling sorry for you

But I ended up feeling sorry for myself
Nothing good in the news these days
Unless it's clapping for the National Health
We keep looking for a crack in the clouds
A breakthrough or a positive sign
Is that a light at the end of the tunnel
Or another train coming down the line.

They're not so sure
Anymore
They're not so sure
They've sailed many times before
But never so far from the shore.

Can you feel the walls closing in
The floor getting closer to the ceiling
The windows are cracking under the strain
The paper on the walls is peeling
They closed another shop in the street today
Broken glass lying in the road
They tell us we are free to leave at last
But there just isn't anywhere to go.

I'm not so sure
Anymore
I'm not so sure
Is there going to be more trouble in store?
If there is.....I can't take any more.

(174) Singing In The Rain - 2020 (page 301)

The Sixties

That first step was a doozy
I mean it really was deep
All hands and knees
All of us falling down in a heap
We had free milk and free time
Idle afternoons blagging chips
Behind the school railing
Playing with iridescent marbles on a drain
Trying to dodge the bullies and failing
Buying pick and mix at the newsagents down the lane
Then going to the dentist to fill in another tooth
While the sky turned indigo above the school roof
Our Mother's held up blue umbrellas
While we held Black Jacks and Fruitellas
Then back home for another dinner out of a can
Sitting at the family table watching Superman
Playing Sergeant Pepper's Lonely Hearts Club Band
We were going to the moon
Or landing on the moon
Or getting our hair done in Vidal Sassoon's
Or living in a commune
It was the sixties, the time of the Beatles and cigarette commercials
It was everything that followed Winston Churchill
Will it ever be like this again?
When we were singing in the rain.

The Seventies

Sitting in the school hall
Waiting to turn over the paper

Being intensely petrified
Of the exam adjudicator
Whether we failed or whether we passed
Whether we stopped writing or whether we had to restart
Our life for a little while would be measured in exam results and marks
We wore brown shorts and scraped our knees
Held buttercups and climbed trees
Eating semolina and strawberry jam
Corn beef, fish fingers and tinned spam
Playing Connect 4 and Ker Plunk
Loving our multi coloured cardboard, plastic and junk
Instant mash and instant karma
Fray Bentos pies and Huntley & Palmer
We were tripping the light fantastic
Getting off on sticky back plastic
Watching Doctor Who and Happy Days
And wandering around in a Purple Haze
We drank Party Seven and Babycham
Whilst failing to understand
Why Guerillas were on the loose in Vietnam
There was trouble in the Lebanon
And trouble in Beirut
We smelt like Henry Cooper
And his great smell of Brut
All the American embassies were under attack
And all the British carpets
Were getting a shake and vac
We were putting the freshness back
There was always something in the air
Or a protest in the wind
Another student demonstration
Or a hippy happening
We were the children of Roy Jenkins and Enoch Powell

Mary Whitehouse and George Brown
Getting off on the notoriety
Of the permissive society
We wore floral shirts
Played progressive rock
Happy to wait in queues and shop
But not everything was rosey so to speak
Coal mining was past its peak
We had the joys of the three day week
Things would get worse
Before they got really bad
Sometimes flower power
Was the only power we had
We were keeping 'em peeled and took care
Suspicious devices were everywhere
Including 22 inch corduroy flares
We watched American dramas in low fi colour
Watergate, Kojak and the Ayatollah
We started holidaying in Spain
We were quirky, rude and vain
But we were singing in the rain.

Then the sky got very grey
Engines stopped running
The dark pits of the north
Gave up the ghost and paused henceforth
No one working the graveyard shift
Decent burials getting short shrift
On the telly, scandal and swearing
A revolution of bondage and spit was flaring
We were at a crossroads but not the motel
Having outgrown glam rock and Mattel
The weight of disappointment feeling crushing

So we went down to Liverpool to do nothing
There was always a harmony in our heads
Leaving our footprints where our parents feared to tread
We were angels with dirty faces
Nut jobs and hard cases
The cause of another trivial headline in the evening paper
Whilst turning a blind eye to "Love Thy Neighbour"
Our parents planned our exorcisms
As we swayed to "rock against racism"
We felt like dogends in the rain
Inadequate participants of the generation game
After a summer of strikes and dissent
Now was the winter of our discontent
And not a prelude to a glorious summer
Well what a bummer
Labour wasn't working, all of us were shirking
Something else in the shadows was lurking
Was it the Lurkers
Or the white collar workers?
Then we heard a rumour
And it wasn't Fleetwood Mac
Our dancing days were over
The Tories were coming back
With vengeance and purpose
But oh what a show and oh what a circus
Don't cry for me Argentina
There she was... blue suit and haughty demeanour
Where there was conflict she would bring division
She was already looking for a place to make her first incision
No more flying paper planes
But we were still singing in the rain.

The Eighties

A drum machine tapped at the back
Of a synthesised soundtrack
To which we enjoyed our workout fads
Eating All-Bran and wearing shoulder pads
We watched Dire Straits on MTV
Loads of us with loads of money
Video had killed the radio star
Now she was working as a waitress in a cocktail bar
We were New Romantics in Vienna
Driving around in our Ford Sierras
Or in our Sinclair C5s
Putting our ZX spectrums into overdrive
We could not be serious and we were delirious
Watching John McEnroe getting overruled
In a tennis psychodrama with Bjorn Borg
Getting very excited about Pizza and curry
Lots of old men in a hurry
Like Menachim Begin
Yuri Andropov and Ronald Reagan
There were new movers and shakers
Richard Branson and Freddie Laker
We were cheering our troops at the battle of Goose Green
For one last time we weren't anachronistic nationalistic hasbeens
War was war and yes people got killed
But it was ok we were only bashing foreigners and Arthur Scargill
We were the objectors and dissenters
To the post war consensus
With savoir faire and bonhomie
We shook hands with the free market economy
Which led to all the Mondays too
The black, the manic and the blue
We sold off nationalised industries

Divided our communities
Buying shares and putting in bids
Making sure we didn't tell Sid
But we were never going to get rich
Join the aristocracy and shoot grouse
Still we could own a council house
Sometimes life felt like a breeze
In spite of mad cow disease
But it was getting overcast and soulless
The cumulus clouds drifting over the faceless
You could feel the weather changing
Things were rearranging
The darker clouds were moving in
Whether it was from a radioactive reactor core
Or another middle eastern war
Or from a new sexually transmitted virus
In this age of the Walkman not the Wireless
The big sky was grey and gusting
And we weren't any good at cloudbusting
Racked by indecision
Our guilty voices had no rhythm
But it hadn't always rained on our parade
Like on that hot day at Live Aid
Or for Helen John at Greenham Common
But it was clear and it was plain
There were fewer of us singing in the rain.

The Nineties

We were climbing over the wall
We were climbing the walls
We were trying to be cool - again
In spite of our European schism
Crashing out of the exchange rate mechanism

A crash course for the ravers
We were welcoming back Labour
Things could only get better
Eating our first bruschetta
Drinking Americanos and Lattes
Planning our millennium parties
We were in a Brit Pop bliss
Getting sorted for E's and Whizz
There were floral reefs outside the palace gates
A princess lying in state
This was the mourning of a nation
In need of education, education, education
But was this what we really really wanted?
As we were still later disappointed
Rosy lips and fools and the burning of a castle
One has had an annus horrible
While those blue boys were still incorrigible
It was getting warmer and the nights were drawing in
And trust the Americans to always win
Who went from building missiles to invading the privacy
Of Hillary Clinton and Monica Lewinsky
With their scandals, cigars and sexual peccadilloes
While the Russians fell from super state to zeroes
Cold War borders consigned to the bin
No more checkpoint Charlie or East Berlin
It was a time of hawks and doves
Like Bush, Kohl and Gorbachev
Nato was the great exploiter
Of Glasnost and Perestroika
We were happy to unpack that gift
And accept it's geopolitical shift
But sadly it could not prevent
Sowing new seeds of discontent

We felt giddy, heady and cloudy
But some spots in the Middle East were a little too rowdy
We'd rocked the Casbah but Sharif didn't like it
So he sold off his weapons of mass destruction to terrorist sidekicks
We still wanted harmony and we still wanted to swing
But we couldn't find a better song to sing
The one we had was shrill and hollow
But something we could all follow
Once you'd heard it you could never get it out of your brain
Not something to be singing in the rain.

The 2000's

We were desperate to go wireless
But we weren't going to worry less
Even though the millennium fallout never materialised
Some bits were going to be worse than we realised
Yes planes would fall out of the sky
We all got bright new devices
We could search and explore
Extrapolate our desires and vices
Open many secret doors
Our pockets filled with smart tech
Wired up and set
Making and remembering passwords
Which we'd spend decades resetting
.....and then forgetting
Envying the sharper and the smarter
And we all wanted to go faster
There was a frenzy
To get virtually friendly
Get your blog or smiley face
On Facebook or MySpace
We embellished ourselves digitally

Nothing had depth or mystery
Unless you could see someone's search history
A world full of links and high jinks
Kittens, pratfalls and embarrassments
Cuddly kids with cute pets
Adult sites and dodgy sex
A billion cappuccino snaps
So much distracting crap
That took time to manage
In an age of brand not brain damage
Leading to many of us feeling marooned
On the dark side of our moon
But we had to be observant too
Be worried about who was in front of you
We packed our kit bags daily
Over our shoulders they swung
On the tube we travelled in silence
We were highly strung
Self conscious nervous wrecks
Trying to be politically correct
And no longer smoking cigarettes
All our coherent conversation
Now a series of texts and notifications
Gossip reduced to a stream of data
We'd all hear about it sooner or later
You didn't need an evening paper
News spreading like feathers
From a million torn pillows
Undulating digital smoke
In tsunami waves and billows
A nuclear rain of information
And misinformation
The start and the creation

Of global dataset saturation
Taking control of every nation
This post millennial hard drive aberration.

2010's

Then the bottom fell out of the money bucket
Those grey civic institutions were crumbling
Bent CEOs were grumbling
This wasn't cricket anymore and no one was holding the bat
We'd relied too heavily on economic technocrats
We had to run and take out our cash
Before the economy crashed
Those money spiders and trade dealing insiders
Who'd been climbing up the spout
Did not see the rain coming which washed them out
Shocking disclosures
Of low standards in high places
Banking closures
No more days at the races
We learnt that no deal is better than a bad deal
But a good deal is better than no deal
And there were a good deal more bad deals than no deals
Which somehow led us to the conclusion
It would be a good idea to leave the European Union
Our Belle Époque was drawing to a close
We were welcoming back the belligerent and bellicose
The party was over and we were clutching at straws
It was about to rain a whole lot more.

We used to fret that a hard rain might fall
Instead we have to suffer the reign of hard fools
We put them there, those Dictaore Perpetuos
With their propaganda and dayglo military shows

Their TV personalities, sound bites and dodgy realities
And let's not pretend we were kept in the dark
We willingly bought from their businesses and financed their oligarchs
Now they preside over floods and forest fires
As the sea levels are getting higher
Oceans flooded with synthetic compounds
We are all becoming water bound
We ignored the experts because their data wasn't thorough
Now we have to suffer the ire of David Attenborough
He didn't start the fire
"Iceberg ahead" - he shouted from the upper deck
Of our self made shipwreck
We were ignorant, breaking nature's rules
By getting shit faced on fossil fuels.

2020 and beyond

......there's something funny going on and it's downright
peculiar
We'll need more than just Robert Downey Junior
We just want to feel better and a little less under the weather
But the damage may already be done
As we bake under an unrelenting sun
A little heat won't hurt you say our indifferent leaders
So why do we hide in the shadows; warmer and weaker?
Procrastinating and creating excuses so lame
I guess we've earnt this sky full of fire and freezing rain.

We used to sing freely and proudly
Whenever bad weather was due
Now all our hopes and fears are in the clouds and all our data is too
We thought we'd survive any flood and never drown
We never thought something so small would bring us down
We thought we'd continue to live without fear of war's disruption

Under the umbrella of our mutually assured destruction
Based on an unholy nuclear alliance
Of uranium and rocket science
We thought we'd said au revoir to the USSR
But now we're reopening those eastern European scars.

Raindrops keep falling on our heads
But these aren't pennies from heaven
Who'll stop the rain?
Where's that glorious feeling
When will we be happy again?
We have rain on Mondays and every other day
And no matter how many times we sing it
The rain just won't go away
Sometimes we laugh at the clouds
Or walk down the lane
Whistling a happy refrain
But wait, listen....
Here comes the rain again.

Stop, hey, what's that sound
Must be Gene Kelly splashing around
The stormy clouds chase everyone from their place
And there's a dark sky above a world lacking in love
Perhaps the rain will always fall and the wind will always blow
And we will always sing and dance on the edge of a volcano
And if the sky becomes ever more darker and dimmer
Then cue oppressive soundtrack, Hans Zimmer.

Once more to the breach dear friends and neighbours
To reach again for those yearning octaves and quavers
Come on now let's make a start
It's always raining in our hearts

Bring your umbrellas, don't be late
Be there ready for the majors, minors and sad middle eight
See the water flowing down the drain
Better get together darlings
We're singing in the rain.

"Come on with your rain,
I've got a smile on my face" *Singin' In The Rain 1952*

(175) We're Getting Warmer - 2020 (page 313)

Shadows pass over an empty town
There used to be crowds, now there's no one around
The sun is so hot it feels like molten steel
No one knows what news is fake or real
We pray we might be turning a corner
We're not there yet
But we're getting warmer.

Something bad is being passed around
It's unpleasant and doesn't make a sound
No one knows from which direction it will come
Half the planet is on the run
Even the prime minister must stand in the global sauna
We're not there yet
But we're getting warmer.

The summer of detente was yesterday
Now it's over the hill and far away
We spy and we lie to keep some semblance of order
We shut doors that should be open and close our borders
Do we have to throw another lamb to the slaughter?
We're not there yet
But we're getting warmer.

Everything we have is out on display
We hide nothing and no one looks away
We face the mirror but don't like what we see
Its out of line with our distracting fantasies
Disappointment now turning to torture
We're not there yet
But we're getting warmer.

For too long we've been playing hide and seek
With either a trend line or a freak
Fixated on our life styles and desires
Not melting ice caps or forest fires
One more false dawn and chorus of Nessun Dorma
We're not there yet
But we're getting warmer.

The mercury is rising and emotions are running high
We try to cover up the latent fear in our eyes
We follow the sound of a brand new battle drum
But we can't remember what it is we're marching from
Over yonder another deadly trauma
We're not there yet
But we're getting warmer.

(176) Hunker In My Bunker 2021 (page 314)

Gonna hunker in my bunker
Like we did in sixty four
Getting ready for disaster
And the next World War
Carving out some "me" time
You might not see me for a while
But I'm happy to have visitors

So come down and make me smile.

Gonna hunker in my bunker
Until this plague has gone
I'm going to write the lyrics
To a brand new protest song
Piling up provisions
Like tins of Campbell's soup
Hydrogenated pizza
And spaghetti hoops.

Gonna hunker in my bunker
I can't get my car downstairs
It doesn't really matter
As I'm not going anywhere
I'm living in my dugout
Just like Saddam Hussein
You won't see me coming up
Until it's safe again.

Gonna hunker in my bunker
With just a book to read
Some satellite telly
And my diary
I've set my notifications
So I know when it's all clear
I wish I was a celebrity
So you could get me out of here.

Gonna hunker in my bunker
Can you tell the United Nations
I'm so stressed and terrified
I'm having palpitations.

It's extremely unseemly
To be away from everyone
But I won't be having visitors
Not even Dad and Mum.

Gonna hunker in my bunker
Crouch down in the mud
I can hear the rain a-pouring
I know here comes the flood
I've had a chat with God
Now I'm working on an ark
When I've got two of everything
I'll be ready to disembark.

Gonna hunker in my bunker
There's not much time to go
The storms they are a-coming
The hurricanes will blow
I won't be stepping out
Until Armageddon's over
And the horsemen of the Apocalypse
Have reached the white cliffs of Dover

And....
... some time in the future....

When I'm feeling older, sadder and drunker
And less happy living down under
With this daylight hunger
Knowing I'm not getting any younger
And just perhaps the world hasn't been torn asunder
By leaders who seek only to plunder
I might get out of this hole and into my car

And pull up to the bumper
But hey it's only a wonder
And I don't want to make a blunder
So for now I'll keep clear of the rain and the delicate sound of thunder
And await a reassuring sign but until that juncture
I'll hunker In my bunker.

(177) Throwaway 2021 (page 317)

When I was a boy, I threw away my toys
Once they lost their novelty
I had my last look then I threw away my books
They no longer interested me
They expected me to pose, so I threw away my clothes
I gave them all to charity
I threw out my LPs and with surprising ease
Then I chucked out my CDs.

There's always one less thing to listen to and one less thing to play
Everything is just a throw away.

I was thrown off my guard by your throwaway remark
So I threw caution to the wind
I threw away my lead when I thought I wouldn't succeed
You made me feel I wasn't performing
I threw you to the wolves when you were heading for a fall
Even though you were struggling
I threw off my mask so you could see the real me at last
All our pretence had been troubling.

You can get rid of anything, no matter what they say
Everything is just a throw away.

When I threw out the baby, I must have been crazy

I was meant to throw out just the bath water
I threw up in a bowl, after I'd completely lost control
Real life felt like torture
You threw me a lifeline when I was alone in the nighttime
After I'd stumbled and I'd faltered
I threw down my tools, after you treated me like a fool
I would show you no quarter.

We covet and discard someone's something everyday
Everything is just a throw away.

She threw the pink bouquet from her wedding display
Hoping some lucky person would catch it
He kept throwing parties, just like Liberace
Each one was unbearable and made a racket
You threw open the door, so you could see me once more
We only had a minute and we had to snatch it
I threw my hat in the ring, I would do anything
If someone was prepared to match it.

If you want to get shot of something, then that's ok
Everything is just a throwaway.

She threw him a sharp stare coupled with a glare
Over the epaulette of her shoulder
He threw a fresh log on the fire and watched the flames get higher
When it was getting a little colder
It threw up strange shadows, as the fire's weary glow
Began to smoke and smoulder
She was thrown into a rage and told him to act his age
When he reached out to try and hold her.

It's rubbish that things don't last or forever stay

Everything is just a throw away.

My inability to just have only what I need
Is really quite appalling
I keep trying to begin, not to chuck stuff in the bin
But I keep procrastinating and stalling
Everything is cheap, there's nothing I need to keep
But who am I fooling
We all just want to grab what we're not entitled to have
Now our world needs overhauling.

What do we want to treasure and what will we save?
Everything is just a throwaway.

(178) All There's Left To Do Is .... SCREAM ☐ - In 2021 (page 319)

Half way through this sentence
Still needing volunteers for clinical trials
Further unrest in China
Asylum seekers walking for miles
Must get a booster for Christmas
The Royals at war with the BBC
A migrant crisis in Dover
Nigella Lawson's Christmas recipes
Strictly Ballroom is over
Inflation now at ten per cent
Cricket's racism crisis
Our money's gone, it's all been spent
The European commission's
Fishing quotas have just increased
No hope of reducing emissions
No zero targets, no press release
Another sleazy manoeuvre
Lobbying for a snout at the political trough

Forecast pandemic statistics
No more new variants please we've had enough
Deliveroo at your doorstep
A cashless shop opens its doors
It's at her majesty's pleasure
But we don't know what we'll use it for
A reduction in capital investment
For the national institute of gene therapy
There's a princess in hiding
And a racist in the royal family
The warmest March on record
Inoculating children just under ten
Thirty nine post office workers
Appeal for justice in court once again

Feeling the squeeze
Nobody's pleased
In fear we freeze
While down on our knees.

Things today are closing in
The past we had is just a dream
Everything is spreading thin
All there's left to do is…. **SCREAM**

Five dead in Wisconsin
Austria back in lockdown as the world spins around
Installing electrical chargers
While deforestation is cutting us down
Australia's relaxing her borders
Thousands lost in a rental scam
More notorious hackers
MPs debate a social welfare plan

Don't take us for granted
Protests happening around Parliament Square
The UK border dilemma
Kim Kardashinan selling new underwear
Gas lines freezing this winter
Rising tariffs cripple those needing care
Online deliveries are booming
Shop closures are happening everywhere
The conditional lockdown is easing
We score zero for our Eurovision Song
A self-driving bus isn't starting
Blame the developers, they got it wrong
Ambulances forced to queue daily
A highly transmissible variant is on its way
Travel rules once more are changing
Looking forward to cancelling our holidays
Violence as protesters rally
For women's rights in new Mexico
We're patrolling French borders
For those desperate people with nowhere to go
A celebrity backs teaching children
Self defence classes in a surreal world
Another feasibility study
To encourage long haul drivers to knit and purl.

Brand new decrees
More costs and fees
In small degrees
We hide our unease.

Things today are closing in
The past we had is just a dream
Everything is spreading thin

All there's left to do is .... **SCREAM** []

Human stem cells in monkeys
More clubs joining the super league
A coup d'état in Mali
Due to some obscure political intrigue
Wildfires are burning
Western Canada is up in flames
Flooding in the border region of Belgium
Kabul airport in the news again
A short range ballistic missile
Lands off the coast of southern Japan
Another North Korean disturbance
The Taliban take over Afghanistan
A new military build up
Like one we'd seen many years before
We're rabbits caught in headlights
There's a boa constrictor knocking on our front door
We're writing missives and papers
Diplomatic emissaries debating in vain
A hard cold Bolshevik winter
Is blowing this way, eastwards again
We seize oligarch assets
But won't endorse a no fly zone
The kill count grows by the hour
But we leave them to stand on their own
Another crisis is looming
Amidst this awful trade in human hope
It's all too consuming
Add another knot to the hangman's rope.

We can't fight the tanks
With just money and banks

We march up the plank
While firing blanks
This sense of unease
That we never appease
We're like refugees
On a boat lost at sea.

Things today are closing in
The past we had is just a dream
Everything is spreading thin
All there's left to do is..... **SCREAM** .

(179) It's Zero Hour - 2022 (page 323)

It's time for leaders, presidents and saints
It's time for protestors with their complaints
It's time for forecasters and statisticians
It's time for astronomers, chemists and magicians
It's time for artists, teachers and writers
It's time for soldiers, marchers and fighters
It's time for kings and queens in power
What time is it? It's zero hour.

It's time for lovers to get out of their beds
It's time for Fathers to help keep us fed
It's time for Mothers to put things right
It's time to do away with stereotypes
It's time for our children to finish their games
It's time for the sick and lonely in pain
It's time for the peacemakers holding their flowers
What time is it? It's zero hour.

It's time for the seasons, from winter to spring
It's time for events and happenings

It's time for earthquakes, volcanoes and floods
It's time for what's in store for us
It's time for the chance to make amends
It's time for the opportunity to start again
It's time for saving our heavenly bower
What time is it? It's zero hour.

(180) UN (under our watch) - 2022 (page 324)

It was unbelievable and unforeseeable
Weren't we unsinkable?
This is the unthinkable
The unflappable said it was unsurprising
The uninformed thought it was unremarkable
We should have been unbeatable and the horrors of the past
unrepeatable
We'd been unworried for so long
About doing business with the unbearable
Who should have been unelectable
But attained unlimited power unopposed
And it was unexpected that this undesirable
Would create such unrest in uncertain times
Things are unravelling and it's unacceptable
We're swimming in uncharted waters
Unhappy and uncomfortable
What's next is unpredictable and we're unprepared
Because he's uncivilised and unethical
His demands unintelligible and peace undetectable
Surrender won't be unconditional unless it's unintentional
Our entente of many years is now undone
We'll now need to unbox the unorthodox
To stop the unstable continuing unimpeded
Committing unmentionables against the unfortunate
Our unofficial response is underwhelming but understandable

The unfaltering are unimpressed
We're slipping unsoundly into the abyss
And can't untangle our way out of this
It's unedifying and unlikely
That we can unburden the innocent
Unless we do something underhand
Which he very much understands
He thinks he's unimpeachable
He's committed the unspeakable
He's unperturbed to the horrors of war and unaffected
Whilst the blameless are over exposed and unprotected
It's unfair, unholy, unlawful, unnecessary, ungodly, unwelcome, unwanted
and it's all happening under our watch.

(181) The King Of Spades - 2022 (page 325)

You could taste the rust and cordite
A smell of copper hanging in the air
Death lying on the floor
Evidence of cruelty everywhere
The aftermath of a blood bath
Following a wicked wrong
The police were taking statements
Or moving the curious along
But he wasn't going anywhere
The King of Spades.

It all started long ago
When his family ruled the local streets
The residents would pay weekly
For shelter and enough food to eat
He massacred the rival gangs
In the spring of thirty six
Enforcing protection payments

With bully boy tactics
And he always had the upper hand
The King of Spades.

His coven of followers
Had ruled for six score years and ten
And they'd fight for a thousand more
So their reign would never end
They wrote a manifesto
Which they nailed to every wall
There were no more non believers
He'd removed them all
Gladly letting fools suffer
The King of Spades.

Chorus

    ...and the band played an arpeggio
    So sad and full of yearning
    In our hearts it's started burning
    It's a refrain we should be learning
    There's a resistance now emerging
    In a protest song....let the band play on.

His domain was never big enough
While there was still another place to take
He hated with a passion
Any other rival on the make
His people on the border
Had a deal with the police
They could get away with murder
This was a fragile peace
And he was the one to break it
The King of Spades.

He said they'd been a skirmish
On the perimeter of their patch
But it was all a lie made up by him
So his master plan could hatch
His men struck in the evening
Before the sun went down
Armed with knives and pistols
They didn't make a sound
Taking no prisoners on order of....
The King of Spades.

As the sun cut the morning clouds
Their invasion was over and complete
And the vanquished had to accept
The terms of their surrender and defeat
His gang rounded up anyone
Who didn't look like them
Laid them all to waste
Even family and friends
There was no one left to argue with....
The King of Spades.

Chorus

    ...and the band played an arpeggio
    So sad and full of yearning
    In our hearts it's started burning
    It's a refrain we should be learning
    There's a resistance now emerging
    In a protest song....let the band play on.

For the border towns and cities
This threat was well understood

But they weren't prepared to do anything
That disturbed the greater good
They negotiated and compromised
So their people didn't suffer
The words they said had little effect
They just sounded tougher
No one was fooling anyone including
The King of Spades.

He reassured his citizens
That this was a defensive operation
That had just one end in mind
To protect the native population
It was safer to believe it
Than to fall from grace
Or end up with a boot or knife
Firmly in your face
He was cruel but never kind
The King of Spades.

The cabal of offended leaders
Couldn't ignore this forever
And soon they'd have to face the truth
And act solidly together
They said they'd face off tyranny
Whatever the risk
They think they have just what it takes
But they don't know where it is
And he never lost anything
The King of Spades.

Chorus
> ...and the band played an arpeggio

So sad and full of yearning
In our hearts it's started burning
It's a refrain we should be learning
There's a resistance now emerging
In a protest song....let the band play on.

A few months later
He reviewed his grand design
Seeking out other streets
To occupy, raise and redefine
He believed his cause and destiny
Was to conquer and acquire
There's always a great deal to do
And five more guns to hire
That's why they called him
The King of Spades.

By the time the clocks go back
And the evening light has turned to dark
His vicious reign may just have ceased
Leaving the truth so cold and stark
We'll review all the evidence
Of his despicable campaign
All his crimes and brutality
Things will never be the same
We know who dug and filled the graves
The King of Spades.

Chorus

...and the band plays an arpeggio
A refrain we still aren't learning
The cities keep on burning
Our back we keep on turning

There's hope that we're not earning
And there's a protest song....but who will sing along?

(182) Spade ♠️ - 2023 (page 330)

If you call a spade ♠️a spade ♠️
Then you may ignore it's worth
For its more than just an instrument
For digging up the earth
Having things in spades
Is great it has been often said
That's because as far as tools go
It's the smartest in the shed
It's used by every builder
For grounding our homesteads
It's midwife to the plants we grow
From every garden bed
It's the darkest playing card
A pointed spearhead
It's the undertakers tool of choice
For burying the dead ♠️

(183) The Day The Earth Caught Fire 2022 (page 330)

It was an old black and white movie from the sixties
About how the world would one day burn
Just a mashup of hokum and science fiction
And starring Leo Mckern
Nuclear tests had tilted the earth
A news team sent to find out who'd done it
A mix of special effects and historic footage
All done on a shoestring budget
Those were the days of grey

When things were so much cooler and duller
In a way I miss those years
In this age of blinding technicolour
Was that movie ahead of its time?
I ponder as the mercury gets higher
Where's the science fiction now I ask
The day the earth caught fire.

The blinds were down, the curtains pulled
Outside felt like an oven
The sun was burning in the sky
It was so hot all of a sudden
Dead flowers hang their heads
While evergreens look exhausted
The smell of burning woodland
Branches brittle and distorted
The sun is searingly brilliant today
Scorching the gardens in my road
Searing my usual palette of colour
With this sensory overload
All halloween oranges and filigree silvers
Like sparks igniting from a pyre
A sun ablaze in a caustic haze
The day the earth caught fire.

The garden is covered in forest cinders
Black ash and burnt amber
Tiny sparks float in the air
Caught in sweeping meanders
The birds burn in the trees
Nothing is making a sound
The young make for the fans
The old cower in their eiderdowns

There are roofs of red hot coals
Under which we're slowly cremated
We simmer in deodorant and sweat
Like spit roasts marinated
Outside there are reports
Of melting wires and burnt tyres
It's not a sin to be staying in
The day the earth caught fire.

You'll need more than sunscreen
If thinking of going out
Forty degree centigrade
Puts an end to climate change doubt
Perhaps we can reverse this trend
All we need is luck
Or is the unpalatable truth
Earth is already fucked
We're getting glazed and basted
Left in our rooms to stew
Or flambéed and grilled
On corporate global barbecues
Taken to the cleaners
And now we're in the dryer
We might not be at war
But this isn't friendly fire
It's not up for discussion
We know where we went wrong
We can't blame Oppenheimer
For this man made weather bomb
What is this then? - the end of days
The second coming of the messiah
The alpha and omega
Or the day the earth caught fire.

"The nations slithered over the brink into the boiling cauldron of war without any trace of apprehension or dismay..."
David Lloyd George

(184) How Does Your Garden Grow? - 2022 (page 333)

Once excited blue hyacinths now lower their floral bells
Burnished sunflowers with their golden apparel aren't doing so well
Purple dahlias and white morning glories
Struggle in this desiccated purgatory
The once loamy clay is arid and thirsty
It can no longer sustain without the rain
The wax begonia and verdant sweet pea
The daffodils are exhausted and ill
Fuchsias magenta and electric should surge
And be the beacon to the hummingbird
We should be snapping snapdragons brilliant red, orange and pink
But they aren't so proud now and bow their heads and shrink
Busy lizzies aren't so busy
Parched, tired and not so pretty
Swaying primrose should rub shoulders
Not burn, wrinkle, droop and smoulder
Purple dashes of dianthus and golden swathes of marigolds
Are not their usual vibrant,dazzling and bold
Where is the palette of pansies in this tumbleweed of dry?
The perennial summer home to newly born butterflies
Luscious lupines are lacklustre
Jubilant geraniums can't find the energy to muster
Or bloom in their clusters
According to the calendar
Mother Nature should be filling her floral canvas
With wild splashes of cyclamen, red and amber
But the baked bone dry garden is proof

The nimbus clouds have abandoned her
And perhaps we have too
Because of the reckless things we have done and continue to do
It's both sad, mad and extraordinary
That like Mary we've been so quite contrary
To the silver bells and cockle shells
Who now are as hot as hell
Or the little maids all in a row
Who departed after their beauty dried up and lost its glow.

What seeds will we now agree to sow?
How on earth in the future will our gardens grow?

(185) The Receivers and the Takers - 2022 (page 334)

Once upon a time....
There were many classes of people
Rich ones and poor ones
Clever ones and stupid ones
Some who took life too seriously
And some who didn't take anything seriously at all.

But all this changed...
After the great plague
And the last war
And the 3rd Great Depression
And the scorching of the earth by our scientific sun.

This left only two classes of people....
The Receivers and the Takers
A new order
The Receivers lived in insulated, protected, spacious and air conditioned apartments
Any environment they desired was just a touch or click away

They had fitness bikes and wall mounted wide screen televisions
They received things all day long; like signals, parcels, applications, posts, comments, likes and tasks
They were shielded and shaded from the storms, the big freezes and the burning heat haze.

The Receivers lived in apartment blocks called 'Hope'
While the Takers lived on streets called 'Despair'
In terraced blocks, dilapidated and chilly
If they couldn't pay their rent then the Receivers would be called in
They hid from heat so extreme that it could melt their unprotected eyes
And cold so intense that it froze their hair until it snapped
The Receivers needed many many Takers to serve their many many needs
They packed them in factories to make and deliver gallons of decaf latte and stitch designer trainers for their feet.

The Receivers never ventured out
As everything they needed was a chat or click away via a virtual friend - like Victoria, Kenny, Lacie and Waldo
They had broadband so fast it could tell them what they wanted before they knew it
While the Takers had wavebands so slow that they could only download work schedules and pornography.

The Receivers received peer to peer virtual payment for coding, processing, planning, consulting and analysing
While the Takers spent their time earning merits in 12 and 24 hour cycles
For picking and sorting and wrapping things the Receivers could keep on receiving
The world was overloaded with Takers who sucked on the remaining kernels of the planet's marrow.

The Receivers spent long days and nights planning the schedules of the Takers

They talked and talked via VR and other synthetic realities about how they could make the Takers' routines tighter, cheaper and more productive for all - but mainly for the Receivers.

The Receivers ate food fresh and varied - made to order and from around the globe

While the Takers ate 'take out' - synthetic fast and hydrogenated.

At Christmas, the Receivers received gifts that were warm and cushy

While the Takers exchanged emojis, game points and chewed hard plastic figurines

The Receivers chatted online endlessly about diversity, ethnicity and sustainability

The Takers only concern was whether they could eat, heat or meet

Or eat heated meat.

The Receivers worked long screen hours .... sometimes so long that their eyes would bleed and their retinas would fall out of their sockets

They were always receiving.....

- ☐ Receiving notifications in the middle of the night
- ☐ Packages and parcels they'd ordered
- ☐ New projects and initiatives to pursue
- ☐ New devices to use
- ☐ New apps and system tools
- ☐ New emojis and programme rules.

While the Takers took everything...

- They took the older Receivers to hospital to clean them up and wipe away the excrement

- They would take the Receivers' rubbish to the utility zone and their shopping to the collection racks

- They would take their sewage to recycling plants
- They would take it on the chin and at a price they would take a willing
Receiver to heaven.
- They took all the heat, all the cold and all the risk
- They took the blame when targets were missed
- They took the last bus home after a day taking shit
- They took all of this day and night until their fingers bled, their feet
swelled and they felt their spinal plates shift
- Deep down they felt the Receivers were taking everything including the
piss.

This went on for years and years....
And then the system went down.

There were many theories as to why this happened
Some thought it was down to Asia or Eurasia or Europa
Some of the Receivers thought it was due to the Takers
The Takers thought it was an act of God
Perhaps in the end it was just one of those things
But either way the phones would no longer, now and then, ping
- The satellites did not talk to the transponders
- The transponders did not talk to the antennas
- The antennas did not talk to the aerials
- The aerials did not talk to the radios
- The radios did not talk to the routers
- The routers did not talk to the devices
- The devices did not talk to the Receivers
And the Receivers did not talk to the Takers.

All the Receivers' lights went off or stayed on until their bulbs popped
They had no one to talk to and nothing to receive
They ran out of coffee and trainers because they couldn't place orders
And the lack of orders created disorder and then chaos.

They dreaded venturing outside their apartments into the cold or the heat
So they stayed in surviving on the last drops of moisture from the air conditioning units and eating the remaining scraps left at the bottom of their eco-friendly refuse sacks.

The Takers were in the dark too
- they had no orders to pack
- no orders to take
- and they received no orders
Soon they would inherit a system devoid of work timetables, points or merits.

They wandered, dazed and confused looking for something to do or someone to blame, occasionally stopping to enjoy the new experience of tormenting a lost Receiver.

In the end the Takers had taken as much as they could take and the Receivers had nothing left to receive.

The world once more was thrown into bedlam and looked to the hand of God, nature or whoever could fix the satellites.

Words Of Hope And Experience

(186) Carry On Living - 2021 (page 340)

Carry on Sergeant
Carry on Nurse
Carry on Williams
Carry on Peter Butterworth
Carry on Windsor
Carry on Jacques
Carry on Cleo
Carry that weight
Carry on Screaming
Carry on Cruising
Carry on Hawtrey
Carry on amusing
Carry on Constable
Carry on Scott
Carry on Cabby
Carry on a lot
Carry on Cowboy
Carry on Dale
Connor, Simms
Douglas as well
Carry on Loving
Carry on Jack
Carry on Abroad
And carry on back
Carry on Doctor
Carry on Spying
Carry on Teacher
Carry on crying
Carry on avoiding losing your head
Carry on being politically incorrect
Carry on regardless
With whatever you do

I just want to carry on living with you.

(187) I'll Be Your Shield - 2022 (page 341)

When the arrows of adversity
Are aimed at your face
And the armies of anxiety
Have invaded your space
The tanks of regret
Drive over your home
The planes of affliction
Overhead have flown
Their missiles of despair
Are now revealed
Then I will be called, to pick up my sword
To fight and not to yield - I'll be your shield.

If the armada of uncertainty
Has sailed into your zone
And it's cannons of sadness
Destroy what you own
The Spanish Inquisition
Won't leave you alone
Now there's no one you trust
They've wire tapped your phone
The spy of resentment
Has your fate sealed
Then I will be called, to pick up my sword
To fight and not to yield - I'll be your shield

When the generals of misfortune
Have rumbled your plan
And you're fighting a battle
No one else understands

The spears of pain
Are denting your pride
The great dictator
Is not on your side
Compassion feels beaten
You're marching up hill
Then I will be called to pick up my sword
To fight and not to yield - I'll be your shield.

(188) A Prayer For Better Days - 2022 (page 342)

May on every Monday
You can live in the most perfect way
May on every Tuesday
You can work, rest and play
May on every Wednesday
You don't let things lead you astray
May on every Thursday
You listen and let everyone have their say
May on every Friday
You move like a dancer in a ballet
May on every Saturday
You keep your procrastinations at bay
May on every Sunday
You bounce back when things are in disarray
May on each and everyday
You make it a little bit more than just ok.

(189) I Can't Do Any Of These Things - 2022 (page 342)

I can't build a cathedral out of my bare hands
I can't make music as good as Sergeant Pepper's Lonely Hearts Club Band
I can't fight injustice or make a courageous stand
I can't toil the fields or nurture this fair land

I can't film a masterpiece about war in Vietnam
I can't make a tapestry from just a hundred strands
I can't make something delicious out of oysters and clams
I can't play tennis and win the Grand Slam
I can't study the universe and tell you how it began
I can't save the environment, I have no master plan
I can't write a comic as good as Spider-Man
I can't be in a popular Japanese boy band
I can't be as funny as Ollie and Stan
I can't pass an Oxbridge medical exam
I can't repair the Great Grand Coulee Dam
I can't deliver what you want from the back of a van
I can't ride a horse across the Rio Grande
I can't teach children to read and understand
I can't lead a rescue mission to Afghanistan
I can't get you the latest 5G broadband
I can't launch my very own fashion brand
I can't learn to play the violin first hand
I can't paint like Monet, Turner or Rembrandt.

I can't do any of these things......but I'm grateful someone can.

(190) Nothing But The Truth - 2023 (page 343)

The search for truth is a noble pursuit
And not trivial to be perfectly honest
You've got to shine a light on what's hidden from sight
You've got to lift up the lid or the bonnet
Why try and pursue something not true
Or when it's veering towards fiction or fallacy
We need to challenge the flaky and anything shaky
Bake everything we say in sharp reality.

None can abide a PowerPoint slide

Full of sound bites the speaker will simply adhere to
Which on further inspection are in need of correction
Because their basis is empty and see through
Every strapline is a just a punchline
Not driven by empirical persuasion
And each stat is dressed just to impress
And won't stack up in robust conversation.

If you don't trust a line quoted in the Times
You shouldn't feel stupid or daft
And avoid the trap of believing the crap
Printed in the Mail or Telegraph
What gets in the press is not there for the best
It's about power and money that's all
And the value of stock, Rupert Murdoch
And his recruitment of bigots and fools.

You don't have to agree with your local Mp
Or the policies he seeks to explain
Who outlines why, he'll stand by your side
But only if you vote him back in again
He explains his plan, so we understand
What in five more years he can do
But all the good things he'll do if he wins
Will have little or no impact on you.

We plan our attack without looking back
As the past always feels like a mystery
So when we do things the, same we can't expect change
As we haven't learnt the lessons of history
Much to our surprise the past can tell lies
But it depends how we want to view it
So we often revise what we thought once were highs

Or when we made a bad call and we blew it

The search for truth is a noble pursuit
If I can be perfectly frank
For in the end, make truth your friend
Not uninformed gaslighted cranks
At close of play if you don't want things grey
Then you better assemble your proof
For all you need to profoundly succeed
Is the truth and nothing but the truth.

(tell the truth and shame the devil)

(191) Compromise - 2022 (page 345)

I wanted a four bed detached
But settled on a two bed semi
I never travelled Virgin business class
Instead I took the train and ferry
I wanted to be the boss
Or a wealthy celebrity
But I accepted my lot
As a middle class non entity
We didn't go away for Christmas
Instead we stayed at home
I couldn't pay off the mortgage
So I took out another loan
I wanted a new car with all the trimmings
Leather seats and alloy wheels
But it was way beyond my budget
So I got one second hand for a cheaper deal
No need for an Apple watch or Phone
When you've got Casio and Motorola
Why celebrate with sparkling Champagne

When you can have lemonade or Coca Cola
You don't need good, better or best
When just ok will do
Why sweat for a first
When I got by on a two two
Better to take a defensive pass
Rather than risk a shot at goal
The family wanted a Labradoodle
But I got them a goldfish in a bowl
From the first day I was born
I knew I wouldn't always get what I wanted
So I made the best of being five foot six
And regularly disappointed.

When all is said and done and not to my surprise
Life's a series of trade offs, I've come to realise
But for all the things I accepted or just didn't do
When it came to love I never compromised on you.

(192) I Just Can't Wait - 2022 (page 346)

I want to sing like a bird and fly like a plane
Shout from the nearest mountain range
Dance in my bedroom with the lights turned out
Dive in a river and mess about
Run to a forest and climb a tree
Buy a big meal for the family
Get a bit tipsy with all my friends
Repeat it all in the morning again
.....and I just can't wait
As I'm already late.

I'm going to put on a pair of platform shoes
Pick up a guitar and play some tunes

And if they have a party next door
I'll ask them to turn the volume up more
Take the kids on a holiday
Pay for their troubles to go away
See my sisters, Mum and Dad
Like I used to when I was a lad.
...and I just can't wait
To avoid my past mistakes.

Have a laugh at work with my mates on zoom
Painting all the elephants in the room
Play truant and bunk off school
Smoke a fag and pretend I'm cool
Drink Merlot in the park
Sleep outside while it's dark
Watch all the Bond films in a row
Mime to Bassey and Matt Munro.
.....and I just can't wait
To do what I haven't done to date.

Sail on a river and run through the trees
I won't let time catch up with me
Travel on a train as far as I can
End up in Brussels or Amsterdam
Take a trip to the home of the blues
Staying in Memphis with a friend or two
Cut some cake and cut some slack
Keep going forward and not look back.
....and I just can't wait
There's just too much at stake.

Jump around with my hands held high
Tear up all my shirts and ties

Take my wife around the globe
Put a stud in my left ear lobe
I won't watch the pounds and pennies
I'll talk nonsense but I won't take any
I'll laugh and cry like a man possessed
Till my heart bursts out of my chest
......and I just can't wait
To middle finger fate.

To err is human to forgive divine
So I'll treat all my rivals to a real good time
What I prepare is what I'll get
So I'm making a bed I won't regret
Trying harder to sustain the planet
But I won't change any of my bad habits
Thank God I'm around to appreciate
All the things I know I need to celebrate
........and I just can't wait
As I'm already late.

Reprise...

I'll gather my shit and polish my act
As the past has a habit of biting back
I won't judge lest I be judged
Life's too short to hold a grudge
There's a place where I need to go
187 Great Cambridge Road
It's the place where I started from
It's where I feel I still belong
With a back garden tucked away
I'm going back there one fine day.

(193) I Want To See The Canyon - 2023 (page 349)

I stayed too long in Knightsbridge
Too many drinks at too many bars
I've been so long in a hurry
Trying to paint a picture of their North Star
They promised me everything
But I was just a slave to their schemes and plans
Now that time is over
I'm going to see the canyon before I pay the man.

I'm told that fear is only
Just the fear of fear itself
I don't hold much to that theory
When I'm so dependent on someone else
I've been too long working for the city
It's a painful truth I now understand
But I don't warrant any pity
I'm going to see the canyon before I pay the man.

I ran too fast on occasions
Trying to catch the last evening train
I really don't need much persuading
To see all that effort was in vain
If you're with me and still travel
Whether you sit or whether you stand
You won't hear me much complaining
I'm going to see the canyon before I pay the man.

She would never tell me
Where it was where she came from
She's no Ruby Tuesday
And I'm the same as everyone
If you've dreams make sure you catch them

Hold them tightly in your hands
And did I forget to mention
I'm going to see the canyon before I pay the man.

I'm going to sleep down in the kitchen
Let the chemicals do their work
I regret my time spent drifting
But at this point to do so feels quite absurd
I've been told my heart is broken
Stretched too far like a rubber band
I'm keeping hid, staying off the grid
I'm going to see the canyon before I pay the man.

(194) A Whole Lot Prettier With You - 2022 (page 350)

I didn't plan to go the long way round
Across such rough uneven ground
Yes, there were snags along the way
And it could be rocky on some days
But it was all a whole lot prettier with you.

I didn't expect so many storms to brew
The sun sometimes struggled to break through
Yes, there was hail and there was snow
But it didn't add much to my woes
As it was all a whole lot prettier with you.

I didn't do all the things I planned to do
Which sometimes made me sad and blue
Yes, my career appointments
Could be a source of disappointment
But they were all a whole lot prettier with you.

I didn't see all the sights I expected to

There was always something else to do
Yes, things got in the way
But there was still beauty in each day
And it was all a whole lot prettier with you.

I didn't expect to listen for so long
To conversations just plain wrong
Unintentional, perhaps
But what I heard was crap
And it was all a whole lot prettier with you.

I've sailed the seas and flown across the sky
I've stood on mountains way up high
Yes, I was often wary
And sometimes the view was scary
But it was all a whole lot prettier with you.

For Sue x

(195) A Life Well Lived (HRH) - 2022 (page 351)

From Winston Churchill to Liz Truss
She's reigned gloriously over all of us
Enjoying each of the many royal pageants and parades
Though I suspect she'd rather have been parachuting with Daniel Craig
She's always been there through trouble, strife and war
For all her citizens including Paddington and Ben Whislaw
There's nothing left now for her to do or give
As we say goodbye to a life well lived.

She's been there to steer and enlighten
Every American president from Harry S. Truman to Joe Biden
Even though in the primaries he should have been royally dumped
She's even entertained Donald Trump

When the sixties were obsessed with drugs and orgies
She cared most about the Windsors and her corgis
No more regrets and no one left to forgive
As we say goodbye to a life well lived.

We have had to accept with a resigned sigh
She'll never say again.... 'My husband and I'
Devoted to duty but distracted by quarrel
She'd get away from it at all at Balmoral
Where she would reside, chasing stag along the glen
Just like Olivia Colman and Helen Mirren
It doesn't matter now who she disagreed with
As we say goodbye to a life well lived.

I'm sure sometimes the role could bring her down
As evidenced in the first season of 'The Crown'
But this didn't stop her uniting our many communities
With her speeches, tours, weddings and jubilees
And she got a lot more things right than wrong
Unlike two Richards, two Edwards one Charles and a John*
To serve her has been both an honour and a privilege
As we say goodbye to a life well lived.

* Also Mary 1st and James 2nd were a bit dodgy too.

(196) The Beauty Of Sadness - 2023 (page 352)

The beauty of sadness
It's in the deep pit of tears behind our eyes
It's the ghost of a lost love we once highly prized
It's great impressions left in albums and frames
Of amazing times that we'll never have again
It's a kind word and a mother's touch
That are lost forever but still mean so much

It's more than respect, more than words, more than duty
The gentlest kiss in the world is the sadness of beauty.

The beauty of longing
Each day we yearn in majestic rainbow swathes
We hope and pray for better more wonderful days
We long for love and feel the ache of hearts being pulled
By dreams of a better half or a darling's future call
We want a loving companion who fits us like a glove
But we've been told many times not to hurry love
To silence this universal refrain would be a matter of cruelty
The greatest song you'll ever sing is to the longing of beauty.

The beauty of grief
A loss so profound and pure it's beyond description and belief
Puccini and Da Vinci couldn't capture its haunting pain and relief
In their gradations of light and shadow and sad motifs
It's more than the obituaries and funeral wreaths
It's an oil painting in a wooden frame of still life, still warm
It's the victory of lasting substance over past form
It's not in prayers, or psalms recited so resolutely
It's in the most awful thief's great release; the grief of beauty.

The beauty of death
Our paintings and stories are defined by our passing
Our unlikeliest kindness is that nothing is lasting
A sky full of blues above an ocean of tears
Wrapped around all the loves and the lives we hold dear
Flowers of fortune all have their day
Their worth not known until they wither away
A hurtful truth that cuts through absolutely
All becomes soaked in sadness and hope with the death of beauty.

(197) The Battle Of Little Book (In A Big Book) - 2023 - (page 354)

Intro to fifteen....
Random acts, bits and pieces
Dug out from my literary creases
A poetic but chaotic load
Of no rhyme or reason or fixed abode.

(i).Leaf

I'm a leaf holding onto a tree
I cling on with all life's energy
But I can't resist the pull
Of mother nature's call
And I'll be withered and gone by Autumn's fall.

(ii).Crows

Three black crows perched on a tree
Dominee Domini
They've flown all the way from purgatory
Dominee Domini
They were the angels of chaos at Babylon and Golgotha
Dominee Domini
Over the planet they maliciously hover
Dominee Domini
They raise hell and high spirits among sisters and brothers
Dominee Domini
It means nothing to them as it's all wooden dollars.

(iii).The Last Surviving Member Of The Dambusters Squad

Another batch of fireworks welcomes a year that's new
While the old one leaves with its baggage and sad end of year
review

A look back on all the happenings, heroes and failures
The broken relationships, faux pas and bad behaviours
Each year we lose something but in this one we've lost a lot
Like the last surviving member of the Dambusters squad.

Last surviving Dambuster George 'Johnny' Johnson dies age 101
8/12/2022 — Mr Johnson was the last surviving original member
of RAF 617 Squadron's famous "Dambusters" raid on the night of
16 May 1943

(iv). Spread

Spread the table
Spread the cheese
Spread your wings
Spread disease
Spread the word
Spread the bed
Spread the love
And spread your legs
Whether you're alive or whether you're dead
Everyone loves a good spread.

(v). I Can't Cry At Funerals

I can't cry at funerals
I just can't cry at all
It's not that I don't want to
Or I'm unemotional
For in my heart I feel profoundly
I know the line that has been crossed
But my tears just can't do justice
To all the passing and the loss
So I won't be crying at funerals

Not now or any time
And if I don't cry at yours
You don't have to cry at mine
(and technically I won't either).

(vi).Welcome To Earth

At the start of the intergalactic holiday season
Earth has many charms and good reasons
For providing a once in a lifetime vacation
As an out of this universe destination .....

We've got dictators and conquerors
And a great selection of universal monsters
We've got disasters, natural and man made
And many viruses; covid, mumps and bubonic plague
You'll find geological disruption
Insider dealing and corruption
Rub shoulders with the unsavoury
Subterfuge and chicanery
You'll see the poor and the sick
In each body politic
And from any view or position
You can see all the machinations of the human condition
We've got floods and forest fires
And our atmosphere is dire
Everything's for hire
You'll never get tired
Of our elevated ambitions and unhealthy desires......

So if you're intending a visit
Whether it's weeks or a few days
Then let us help you plan your journey
And find a great place to stay

But before starting your adventure
Your bags will need a search
We've got enough suspicious devices, thank you
Welcome to Earth.

(vii). King

Carrie, Cujo and Christine
Are living it up with Stephen King
You never know what misery will bring
So they're taking a stand against all the needful things.

(viii). Larkin

They fuck you up your, Mum and Dad
As Philip Larkin said
And if they don't it's likely that
Your children will instead.

(ix). Leave

I didn't ask to come into this world
It wasn't me who decreed it
And when it's getting time to go
I won't be asked when I want to leave it.

(x). Younger

I know what I want to be when I get older
Younger.

(xi). I Love The End Of Something Bad

I love the end of something bad
Especially when it's dreadful

I love the ending of despair
When I no longer feel so fretful
I love the end of bad conditions
Any period of disorder
I love it when the worst has passed
And I have turned a corner
I love to close off a bad patch
And that feeling of relief
When I can finally sleep at night
And wave goodbye to grief
I love the end of something bad
When it looks like I've survived
And that awful time has passed
And it feels good to be alive.

(xii). Weaponise (#12 & 35)

They'll weaponise a peace after a war
They'll weaponise the food in the grain stores
They'll weaponise our friends and then their pets
They'll even weaponise the internet
But this shouldn't come as a big surprise
Anything can be weaponised.

They'll weaponise the sea and open sky
They'll weaponise the truth and then the lies
They'll weaponise the news and books we read
They'll weaponise the very air we breathe
But this shouldn't come as a big surprise
Anything can be weaponised.

They'll weaponise the churches and the priests
They'll weaponise every press release
They'll weaponise the data on our phones

They'll weaponise the gadgets in our homes
But this shouldn't come as a big surprise
Anything can be weaponised.

They'll weaponise the canvas and the screen
They'll weaponise the soap that keeps us clean
They'll weaponised the colour of our skin
They'll weaponise the first original sin
But this shouldn't come as a big surprise
Anything can be weaponised.

They'll weaponise our children all by stealth
They'll weaponise the cost of national health
They'll weaponise the wages that we're paid
They'll weaponise good causes and crusades
But this shouldn't come as a big surprise
Anything can be weaponised.

(xiii). Tick Tock

I will set my people free
                    Tick Tock, Tick Tock
From our eastern border to the southern sea
                    Tick Tock, Tick Tock
I'll defeat our enemies
                    Tick Tock, Tick Tock
And grow our wealth and economy
                    Tick Tock, Tick Tock
I'll build Olympic stadiums
                    Tick Tock, Tick Tock
Ice rinks and palladiums
                    Tick Tock, Tick Tock
You'll corral around my worthy goals
                    Tick Tock, Tick Tock

But I will keep complete control
                    Tick Tock, Tick Tock
You might not always be fond of me
                    Tick Tock, Tick Tock
But I'm better than having anarchy
                    Tick Tock, Tick Tock
Then I'll the reach out to our friends and neighbours
                    Tick Tock, Tick Tock
Offering them many trading favours
                    Tick Tock, Tick Tock
They will love my cultural parades
                    Tick Tock Tick Tock
I'm the best new friend they've made
                    Tick Tock, Tick Tock
With a production line that never quits
                    Tick Tock, Tick Tock
Turning out the good stuff and the shit
                    Tick Tock, Tick Tock
I will smile and shake their hand
                    Tick Tock, Tick Tock
But behind their back make other plans
                    Tick Tock, Tick Tock
Building up a network tree
                    Tick Tock, Tick Tock
Of all their threats and enemies
                    Tick Tock, Tick Tock
I know they love technology
                    Tick Tock, Tick Tock
So I'll provide them tech for free
                    Tick Tock, Tick Tock
I will know what makes them tick
                    Tick Tock, Tick Tock
I'll own their data and all they click

Tick Tock, Tick Tock

I'll also provide them low cost loans
Tick Tock, Tick Tock

And the cheapest mobile phones
Tick Tock, Tick Tock

Plus all the WiFi for their homes
Tick Tock, Tick Tock

But my real plans won't be known
Tick Tock, Tick Tock

And anyway the seeds are sown
Tick Tock, Tick Tock

Now my cause can't be postponed
Tick Tock, Tick Tock

To take every single thing they own
Tick Tock, Tick Tock

Then their regime will disappear
Tick Tock, Tick Tock

While mine will last for a thousand years
Tick Tock, Tick Tock.

(xiv). Please Delete Me ♪♪♪

Please delete me let me go
Because you don't love me anymore
To share my posts with friends is not ok
So delete me off your Facebook page.

You have found a new love I now know
It was on your status update a week ago
There's a photo of you sitting on his lap
A week after you used a dating app.

Please delete me can't you see

It's easy to do this digitally
I'm on your site now just for show
So delete me and darling let me go!

(xv). Illusion

Feeling disillusioned
Comes from living an illusion
So I've recently concluded
All my life I've been deluded.

The End Of Little Book

(198) Has Anything Gone? -2023 - (page 362)

In olden days we just played vinyl
We won the World Cup final
So what went wrong?
Has anything gone?

We enjoyed the sun without applying factor
And nobody's pronoun ever mattered
Blame Erica Jong
Has anything gone?

Nowadays
We're so uptight today
About what's right to say
There's just shades of grey
In a smoky haze
Please avert your gaze
Oh what a carry on.

You could stay out late and not feel threatened

Get home when the sun was setting
And cruise along
Has anything gone?

Pop artists had innate ability
They were liked but kept their credibility
Writing songs
Has anything gone?

Now it's AI today
And WiFi today
Spotify today
Or Prime today
We can lie today
But pass it by today
And still think we get along.

We weren't addicted to social media
But things could be whole lot seedier
And we didn't cotton on
Has anything gone?

Something deemed to be too shocking
Was on the top shelf when we went shopping
With just a hint of blonde
Has anything gone?

Now there's porn to view
In a second or two
It can of me and you
And the neighbours too
And be awfully rude
But we're not prudes

And don't care where it's from.

We always talked about the weather
Conversation we would treasure
We smiled when the sun shone
Has anything gone?

We took comfort in a Cold War neutrality
But also knew the harsh finality
Of the neutron bomb
Has anything gone?

It's safe to say
We invade today
And we take today
What's not ours today
We waste away
We're a weaker kind today
No longer global paragons.

We thought we would fly around the galaxy
But that giant step turned out to be fallacy
One step beyond?
Has anything gone?

When did we stop all our hopeful thinking
To become permanently scared and sinking
What on earth's gone wrong?
Has anything gone?

(Thank you Cole Porter for the inspiration)

(199) You Have The Right To Remain Silent - 2023 (page 365)

You have no life
You have no friends
We know your troubles
Will never end
You've no ambition
None at all
You can't fix this
We took your tools
We're putting a stop to the stuff you're sent
But you still have the right to remain silent.

You have no wheels
We took your car
It's pretty clear
You won't go far
You've got more wrong
We've got more right
You're in the dark
We work the lights
We know your money has all been spent
But you still have the right to remain silent.

We took your cover
Now you're exposed
You have no plan
And nowhere to go
You have no vision
You have no goals
No social welfare
Or begging bowl
We've shut all the places you used to frequent
But you still have the right to remain silent.

You have no one
That's on your side
You have no tears
They've all been cried
There is no office
Or governing board
Who'll intervene
You're overruled
You can't even protest or repent
But you still have the right to remain silent.

(200) How Does It Feel? - 2023 - (page 366)

How do you know someone loves you?
Is it when they say you're the one
Why does the world keep on turning?
How do we follow the sun?
What is the meaning of reason?
How do we know when we're ill?
Why must there be changing seasons
And how does it feel?

Why do we close all our borders?
How does a bird learn to fly?
Why do we keep writing sad songs?
Why must we shut down and die?
Why does the clock keep on ticking?
Piling up time to be killed
Why is there still something missing?
And how does it feel?

Why are some days amazing?
I glow when I hold your hand

Why have I not always treasured?
Each moment with you that I can
Why am I destined to leave here?
I can never be happy and still
Why do things have an ending?
And how does it feel?

(201) Until The Next Good Time - 2022 (page 367)

We'll hear again the clinking of bottles and popping of corks
The clattering of stainless steel knives and forks
Once more we'll all be called to make a celebratory toast
After one more family gathering around a Sunday roast
We'll enjoy again our ice cream cones together at the village green
We'll sip sangria in another far off location, sun drenched and serene
So let's look forward to the next happening sublime
Come on, raise your glasses to the next good time.

We'll pack our bags and travel to a destination abroad
We'll all do amazing things for unexpected rewards
Perhaps another carafe of wine shared over an italian meal
Or buy something we've always wanted for one more crazy deal
We'll see another classic movie which we'll afterwards discuss
Reenact the best scenes travelling home on the bus
Let's look forward to leaving all our troubles well behind
Come on, raise your glasses to the next good time.

We'll gather at Christmas around frosty trees and lakes
We'll exchange once more reunion hugs, kisses and handshakes
We'll plan and book our secret sunshine winter breaks
Or blow the candles out on another well iced birthday cake
We'll stand again on mountain tops towering way up high
We'll feel again like angels that can nearly touch the sky
Listen to one more rock masterwork that leaves us awe inspired

That has us dancing round our rooms charged up, pumped and fired
Let's look forward to one more opportunity to unwind
Come on, raise your glasses to the next good time.

When next we're faced with challenges we didn't expect
We're anxious and we're worried and feel like nervous wrecks
Or cause time is passing and we can't ever bring it back
It's like nothing is for us and the odds against us stacked
When we wish we weren't ourselves but someone else instead
Or all we want to do is disappear in our dishevelled beds
Then it's time to let hope shine through these bouts of dread
If we can last, this will pass and there'll be better times ahead
So let's look forward to the dark sky unveiling brighter signs
Come on, raise your glasses to the next good time.

Thank You

mfishman@oblivion.com

Much love to Sue, Emily and Matthew - everyone of my Friends and Family ....and the others.

The End

Printed in Great Britain
by Amazon